All Color Book of
PARTY
COOKING

All Color Book of
PARTY
COOKING

ARCO PUBLISHING INC.
New York

CONTENTS

Series editor: Mary Lambert

Published 1984 by
Arco Publishing, Inc.
215 Park Avenue South
New York, NY 10003

© Marshall Cavendish Books Limited 1984

Library of Congress
Catalog Card Number: 84-70833
ISBN 0-668-06218-5 cloth
ISBN 0-668-06225-8 paper

Printed in Italy

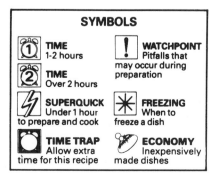

SYMBOLS

🕐 **TIME**
1-2 hours

! **WATCHPOINT**
Pitfalls that may occur during preparation

🕑 **TIME**
Over 2 hours

⚡ **SUPERQUICK**
Under 1 hour to prepare and cook

✳ **FREEZING**
When to freeze a dish

⏱ **TIME TRAP**
Allow extra time for this recipe

ECONOMY
Inexpensively made dishes

INTRODUCTION

Entertaining family and friends can be fun; but it can also involve a great deal of time and expense. It need not be so, *Party Cooking* shows you how entertaining can be economic and fun for the busy cook. There are full three-course menus for each meal with detailed planners on when to prepare each course. Each meal is attractively illustrated in full color so that you can see the finished effect. Menus have been planned with an international flair — treat your friends to a Mexican evening, for example, and those special occasions like a romantic Valentine's dinner for two or entertaining friends at a New Year's party are also catered for. A more formal cocktail party menu is also included and special birthday and party meals just for the kids.

If you really need to cook to a strict budget or are in a hurry, several menus on this theme have been included.

All the recipes contain cook's notes which give you serving and buying ideas for each dish. They are calorie-counted and also tell you the timing of the particular course and alternative ideas to make the dish more economic or perhaps more exotic.

MEXICAN EVENING

Throw an exciting buffet party centered around two savory dishes that are made with tortillas, the famous Mexican crêpes: Chicken enchiladas and Beef tacos. Start with a tequila cocktail, and finish with a pineapple pudding to complete the exotic flavor.

Flour tortillas

MAKES 12
2 cups all-purpose flour
1 teaspoon salt
1 teaspoon baking powder
1 tablespoon shortening, diced
¾ cup water

1 Sift the flour, salt and baking powder into a bowl. Add the fat and cut it slowly and carefully into the flour until the mixture resembles fine bread crumbs. Mix in the water to form a stiff dough.
2 Divide the dough into 12 pieces and shape into balls. Roll each ball out thinly on a lightly floured surface to form 4-inch rounds.
3 Put an ungreased heavy-based skillet over moderate heat until hot, then add a dough round and cook 2 minutes on each side until lightly flecked with brown. Wrap tortilla in a dish towel. ⓘ
4 Fry remaining rounds adding them to the dish towel as they are cooked (see Cook's tip).

Chicken enchiladas

SERVES 6
12 warm tortillas
1 lb boneless cooked chicken, shredded (see Buying guide)
vegetable oil, for frying
½ cup grated Parmesan cheese

SAUCE
1 can (about 4 oz) jalapeño peppers, (see Buying guide)
1 small onion, roughly chopped
1 can (about 14 oz) tomatoes
2 tablespoons vegetable oil
1 large egg
1 cup heavy cream
salt
about 2 tablespoons chicken broth

1 Make the sauce: Rinse the peppers under cold running water, pat dry, then chop roughly. Purée the peppers, onion and tomatoes in their juice in a blender until smooth.
2 Heat the oil in a skillet, add the purée and cook over moderate heat, stirring constantly 3 minutes. Remove pan from the heat.
3 Beat the egg with cream, and salt to taste.
4 Gradually stir the cream mixture into the cooked purée. Return the pan to low heat and cook, stirring, 1 minute. If sauce is too thick, thin slightly with chicken broth. Remove from heat; set aside.
5 Put the shredded chicken into a bowl and stir in 2-3 tablespoons of the sauce to moisten it. Set aside.
6 Preheat the oven to 350°.
7 Fill a heavy-based skillet with oil to a depth of ½-inch and heat over moderate heat. When the oil is sizzling, add a tortilla and fry for a few seconds on each side. Lift out with tongs and dip into the sauce, which should still be warm.
8 Place the sauce-coated tortilla in a shallow ovenproof dish, about 12 × 8 inches. Put a spoonful of the chicken mixture onto the tortilla, then fold in half.
9 Cook, dip and fill the remaining tortillas in same way, arranging them neatly in the dish. Pour over the remaining sauce, then sprinkle with cheese.
10 Bake 20 minutes.

Beef tacos

SERVES 6

12 warm tortillas

BEEF FILLING

1 lb lean ground beef
2 tablespoons vegetable oil
1 onion, finely chopped
1 clove garlic, crushed
1 can (about 8 oz) tomatoes
2 teaspoons chili powder
½ teaspoon ground cumin
½ teaspoon dried oregano
salt

1 Make the beef filling: Heat the oil in a skillet, add the onion and cook gently 5 minutes until soft and lightly colored. Add the garlic and continue to cook about a further 2 minutes.

2 Add the beef and cook briskly, stirring with a wooden spoon to remove lumps, about 5 minutes until the meat is evenly browned.

3 Stir in the tomatoes with their juice, the chili powder, cumin, oregano and salt to taste. Bring to a boil, then lower the heat and simmer, stirring, about 20 minutes until the meat is cooked.

4 To serve: spoon a little beef filling into the tortilla, then fold over and eat with your fingers (see Serving ideas).

Flour tortillas

 TIME
The tortillas take 1 hour to make in total.

WATCHPOINT
Keep the tortillas warm in a dish towel, so that they remain soft and pliable and do not crack when folded.

COOK'S TIP
These tortillas can be made up to 45 minutes in advance: wrap them, still in the dish towel, in foil and keep warm in an oven heated to 225°.

DID YOU KNOW
Tortillas of this type are very popular in northern Mexico where they are known as *Tortillas de harina del norte*. The other kind of tortillas famous to Mexico use a special flour, *masa harina*, which is made from boiled maize. Traditionally they are cooked on an ungreased griddle called a *comal*.

● 80 calories per tortilla

Chicken enchiladas

 TIME
About 1 hour to prepare and cook.

BUYING GUIDE
2 lb cooked chicken yields about 1 lb meat. Jalapeño peppers are sold in larger supermarkets.

● 580 calories per portion

Beef tacos

 TIME
The beef filling takes 35 minutes to make.

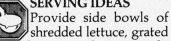 **SERVING IDEAS**
Provide side bowls of shredded lettuce, grated cheese, guacamole (avocado dip), finely chopped onion and bottled taco sauce or any other hot chili sauce. Each person can then add a little of each to the beef filling before folding.

As an appetizer, serve tortilla chips, if wished, to dip into the taco sauce.

● 340 calories per portion

Acapulco pineapple pudding

SERVES 6
½ lb pound or white cake
3 tablespoons apricot jelly
1¼ cups dairy sour cream
½ cup slivered almonds,
   toasted

PINEAPPLE SAUCE
1 can (about 13 oz) crushed
   pineapple
¾ cup sugar
½ cup ground almonds
4 egg yolks, lightly beaten
generous pinch of ground cinnamon
½ cup dry sherry

1 Make the sauce: Put the pine-apple with its juice in a saucepan with the sugar, almonds, egg yolks, cinnamon and half the sherry. Stir with a wooden spoon until the ingredients are well mixed.
2 Place the pan over very low heat and cook, stirring constantly, about 5 minutes or until the sauce has thickened. Set aside to cool about 15 minutes.
3 Meanwhile, split the cake into three layers, then spread cut cake into fingers with the apricot jelly.
4 Arrange half the sponge cakes, jelly side up, in a glass serving dish large enough to hold the cakes in a single layer.
5 Sprinkle with half the remaining sherry, then spread half the pine-apple sauce over the top. Repeat these layers once more, using the remaining sponges, sherry and sauce. Refrigerate 2-3 hours.
6 Remove the pudding from the refrigerator and spread dairy sour cream over the top. Sprinkle the surface with the toasted almonds and serve at once.

CHINESE MEAL

For an exotic change, try making a Chinese meal – it will provide an interesting break from the more usual diet and eating traditions. The ginger-flavored fried shrimp appetizer has to be eaten with the fingers to be enjoyed, while the glazed pork is fun to eat with chopsticks. The meal ends on a light refreshing note with delicately flavored fruit salad.

Gingered deep-fried shrimp

SERVES 6
1 lb large shrimp
  (see Buying guide)
vegetable oil, for frying

BATTER
½ cup all-purpose flour
¼ teaspoon salt
1 egg
⅔ cup water
1 teaspoon chopped root ginger
¼ teaspoon freshly ground black
  pepper

1 Peel the shrimp, then make a shallow cut down the center back of each shrimp and gently scrape away the black vein with the point of a knife. Rinse well, then pat dry.
2 Make the batter: Sift the flour with the salt into a bowl and make a well in the center. Beat the egg with the water, pour into the well and, using a wire whisk, gradually draw the flour into the liquid. When all the flour is incorporated, beat well, then beat in the ginger and pepper.
3 Fill a skillet with oil to a depth of ¾-inch and put over moderate heat. When the oil is on the point of smoking, dip a few shrimp in the batter: coat well with batter, then drop into the hot oil.
4 Cook the shrimp for 1 minute on each side, until the batter turns golden brown. Transfer with a slotted spoon to a serving platter; keep hot while cooking the rest.
5 Serve hot, accompanied by dips (see Serving ideas).

Marinated roast pork

SERVES 6
3 lb pork tenderloin, cut into 6-inch
  lengths
3 tablespoons sunflower or
  groundnut oil
3 tablespoons honey
shredded lettuce, to garnish

MARINADE
5 tablespoons soy sauce
3 tablespoons medium-dry sherry
1½ tablespoons brown sugar
2 cloves garlic, crushed
½ teaspoon freshly ground black
  pepper
½ teaspoon salt
½ teaspoon mixed dried sage and
  thyme
¼ teaspoon ground cinnamon

1 Place the pork lengths in a single layer in a deep dish.
2 Make the marinade: Beat the marinade ingredients together until thoroughly combined.
3 Pour the marinade over the pork and leave to marinate at least 2½ hours, turning occasionally.
4 Preheat the oven to 425°. Remove the pork from the marinade with a slotted spoon, reserving the marinade. Place the pork on a rack in a roasting pan.
5 Roast the pork in the oven 15 minutes, then remove from the oven and reduce the oven temperature to 350°. Brush the pork with the reserved marinade and the oil to coat thoroughly, then return to the oven a further 10 minutes.

6 Just before the end of the cooking time, warm the honey in a small pan over low heat. Remove the pork from the oven, brush with the warmed honey, then return to the oven to roast a further 5 minutes.
7 Cut the pork crosswise into ¼-inch thick slices. Serve hot, garnished with shredded lettuce.

Fried rice

SERVES 6
2¼ cups long-grain rice, boiled
5 tablespoons vegetable oil
1 large onion, chopped
⅓ cup frozen peas
½ green pepper, seeded and diced
1 cup shredded lettuce
1 tablespoon soy sauce
salt and freshly ground black
  pepper

1 Heat 3 tablespoons of the oil in a large skillet, add the onion and cook gently 5 minutes until soft and lightly colored.
2 Add the peas, green pepper and lettuce, stir 1 minute, then push to the side of the pan.
3 Pour the remaining oil into the center of the pan, heat gently, then add the rice and cook 1 minute, stirring. Draw the vegetables from the sides of the pan into the rice and stir together.
4 Stir in the soy sauce, then add salt and pepper to taste. Remove the pan from the heat and continue to stir for a further minute off the heat. Transfer to a warmed dish.

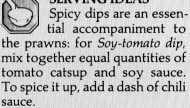

Cook's Notes

Gingered deep-fried shrimp

TIME
Preparation and cooking take 30 minutes.

BUYING GUIDE
The king-sized shrimp suitable for this dish may be fresh or frozen (thaw before peeling), and can be of various species. Shrimp deteriorate quickly so use as soon as thawed.

SERVING IDEAS
Spicy dips are an essential accompaniment to the prawns: for *Soy-tomato dip*, mix together equal quantities of tomato catsup and soy sauce. To spice it up, add a dash of chili sauce.
  For *Soy-mustard dip*, mix 1 part English mustard with 2 parts soy sauce.

● 105 calories per portion

Marinated roast pork
TIME
2½ hours marinating, 30 minutes cooking.

● 420 calories per portion

Fried rice
TIME
20 minutes for boiling rice, then 15 minutes.

● 330 calories per portion

Oriental fruit salad

SERVES 6
1 small honeydew
   melon
1 can (about 11 oz) mandarins,
   drained
¼ cup medium-dry
   sherry
1 can (about 1 lb) lychees

1 Cut the melon in half and scoop out the pits. Cut the flesh into balls using a melon baller, then put in a glass bowl.
2 Add the drained mandarins and sherry to the melon, then pour the lychees, together with their juice, into the bowl.
3 Stir the fruit gently, cover and refrigerate 2 hours before serving.

Cook's Notes

TIME
This delicately-flavored fruit salad only takes 15 minutes preparation, plus chilling time.

VARIATION
Use fresh mandarins and lychees when in season and substitute the canned lychee juice with a sugar syrup: Dissolve ¼ cup sugar in ⅔ cup water, add the sherry, then boil the syrup mixture for 2-3 minutes. Leave the syrup to cool completely before mixing with the fruit.

The sherry in the salad may be replaced by dry white wine, or, for added zing, by an orange liqueur, such as Cointreau.

● 110 calories per portion

COUNTDOWN
In the afternoon
● Marinate the pork for the Marinated roast pork.
● Boil the rice for the Fried rice.
● Make the Oriental fruit salad and refrigerate.
1½ hours before
● Prepare the vegetables for the Fried rice.
● Peel the shrimp and refrigerate.
● Make the accompanying dips for the Gingered deep-fried shrimp.
45 minutes before
● Heat the oven.
● Make the batter for the shrimp.
30 minutes before
● Start roasting the pork.
● Fry the shrimp; keep hot.
15 minutes before
● Reduce the oven temperature, baste the pork and continue to roast.
● Make the Fried rice.
5 minutes before
● Baste the pork with honey; continue to roast. Slice before serving.

CARIBBEAN-STYLE DINNER

The colorful atmosphere of the Caribbean is captured in this exciting menu for six. The flavors that are the very essence of West Indian cookery feature strongly in every dish, and the choice of three sensational cocktails really makes the meal!

Piña colada

MAKES 6 LONG DRINKS
3 cups unsweetened pineapple juice
1¼ cups canned coconut cream (see Buying guide)
1½ cups white or golden rum
plenty of crushed ice

1 Quarter fill a pitcher with ice, add one-third of the ingredients and mix briskly. Or blend for 2-4 seconds in a blender.

2 Pour into 2 chilled glasses and serve at once. Mix up 2 more batches with the remaining ingredients.

Caribbean blues

MAKES 6 SHORT DRINKS
1½ cups vodka
⅓ cup blue Curaçao
⅓ cup dry vermouth
plenty of crushed ice, to serve

1 Put all the ingredients, except the ice, in a large pitcher and mix well.
2 Fill 6 chilled cocktail glasses with crushed ice, pour the cocktail over the ice and serve at once.

Planter's punch

MAKES 6 LONG DRINKS
1½ cups dark rum
¾ cup lemon juice
4 teaspoons grenadine
1¼ cups orange juice
1¼ cups pineapple juice
few dashes of Angostura bitters
plenty of crushed ice, to serve

TO GARNISH
6 orange slices
6 lemon slices
6 cocktail cherries

1 Put all the ingredients, except the ice, in a large pitcher and stir well.
2 Fill 6 large glasses with crushed ice and pour the punch over the ice. Garnish each glass with an orange and lemon slice and a cherry.

Cook's Notes

Piña colada

TIME
20 minutes preparation in total.

BUYING GUIDE
Canned coconut cream is available in some large supermarkets, but if you find it difficult to obtain, use a 6 oz block creamed coconut and dissolve it in about 1¼ cups hot water. Creamed coconut is available from most supermarkets, and shops specializing in Indian food.

DID YOU KNOW
The name piña colada means soaked pineapple in Spanish.

● 365 calories per glass

Caribbean blues

TIME
5-10 minutes preparation in total.

COOK'S TIP
To make crushed ice: Crush ice cubes in a strong blender or in a food processor. If you do not have either, place the ice in a strong plastic bag, squeeze out the air and tie firmly. Place the bag on a folded dish towel and beat with a rolling pin until the ice is reduced to fragments.

● 160 calories per glass

Planter's punch

TIME
5 minutes preparation in total.

● 170 calories per glass

West Indian fish patties

①

SERVES 6

½ lb cod fillets
1 tablespoon wine vinegar
1¼ cups cold water
1 tablespoon vegetable oil
½ small onion, chopped
¼ red pepper, seeded and chopped
2 tablespoons chopped parsley
2 tablespoons canned chopped
    tomatoes
juice of ½ lemon
3 dashes hot-pepper sauce
salt and freshly ground black
    pepper
1½ sheets (¾ of 17 oz package)
    frozen puff pastry, thawed
1 egg white, lightly beaten

1 Put the fish in a heavy pan with the vinegar and water, bring just to a boil, then lower the heat slightly and simmer gently 10 minutes.
2 Drain the fish and, when cool enough to handle, skin, bone and flake the flesh.
3 Heat the oil in a pan, add the onion and cook gently 5 minutes until soft and lightly colored. Add the red pepper and parsley and cook a further 5 minutes.
4 Add the flaked fish, together with tomatoes, lemon juice, pepper sauce, salt and a generous sprinkling of pepper. Simmer, uncovered, stirring occasionally, a further 10-12 minutes until most of the liquid has evaporated. Transfer to a bowl, taste, adjust seasoning and leave to cool.
5 Roll out the pastry: the large sheet to a 16 × 8 inch rectangle and the small sheet to an 8 inch square.
6 Preheat the oven to 425°.
7 Cut the pastry into twelve 4-inch squares. Place a portion of the fish mixture in the center of each square, then lightly dampen the pastry edges with cold water and fold each square into a triangle. Press the edges together, then crimp with a fork to seal well.
8 Arrange the patties well apart on 2 cookie sheets and brush the surfaces with egg white, then prick each patty with a fork 2-3 times. Bake in the oven about 20 minutes until golden brown.

Pork roast with rum

SERVES 6

②

4½ lb pork loin on the bone
1 teaspoon salt
1 teaspoon ground ginger
½ teaspoon freshly ground
    black pepper
½ teaspoon ground cloves
3 cloves garlic, crushed
3 bay leaves
2½ cups chicken broth
¾ cup dark rum
⅔ cup firmly packed light brown
    sugar
4 tablespoons lime juice
1 tablespoon all-purpose flour

1 Using a very sharp knife, score the skin of the pork fairly deeply, almost through to the fat, in a diamond pattern.
2 Preheat oven to 325°.
3 Pound the salt, ginger, pepper, cloves and garlic to a paste in a mortar and pestle. Rub the paste well into the scored surface of the pork; place bay leaves on top.
4 Pour about ⅔ cup of the broth into a roasting pan, together with one-third of the rum. Put the meat, skin-side up, on a rack in the pan and roast in the oven 1 hour.
5 Meanwhile, mix the brown sugar, lime juice and remaining rum in a bowl.
6 Remove the meat from the oven and baste with the sugar and lime mixture. Return the meat to the

oven and continue to roast a further 1¼ hours. Add more broth to the pan during this time, if the liquid appears to be drying out.

7 Transfer the meat to a warmed serving platter and discard the bay leaves. Keep the meat hot.

8 Pour off the liquid from the roasting pan into a jug, skim off the excess fat and return 1 tablespoon to the roasting pan Place the pan on top of the cooker and sprinkle in the flour. Stir over low heat 1 minute, then stir in the remaining broth and the reserved cooking liquid. Simmer, stirring constantly, until the sauce has thickened. Season to taste with salt and pepper, transfer to a warmed sauceboat and hand separately.

West Indian fish patties

 TIME
Making the filling and assembling the patties takes about 1 hour, while cooking in the oven takes 20 minutes.

 BUYING GUIDE
An excellent alternative to hot-pepper sauce is Picka-peppa sauce which is found in shops specializing in West Indian food. This is sweet as well as hot: about ¼ teaspoon is enough.

● 325 calories per patty

Pork roast with rum

 TIME
15 minutes preparation, plus 2¼ hours cooking.

 BUYING GUIDE
Ask the butcher to chine the loin — cut through the backbone.

 SERVING IDEAS
Serve fried, sliced plantains or bananas as a side dish — they provide a smooth-flavored contrast to the rich, spicy pork.

● 1105 calories per portion

Coconut soufflé

SERVES 6

 1½ cups canned coconut cream (see Buying guide)
6 eggs, separated
⅓ cup superfine sugar
1½ envelopes unflavored gelatin
4 tablespoons cold water
2 limes (see Preparation)
1 cup unsweetened shredded coconut

1 Put the coconut cream into a pan and gently bring almost to simmering point. Remove from the heat and set aside.
2 Put the egg yolks and sugar in a heatproof bowl that will fit over a pan of water. Beat together until thick and pale, then stir in the warmed coconut cream until thoroughly mixed in.
3 Set the bowl over a pan of barely simmering water and cook, stirring constantly, about 10 minutes until the mixture is smooth and slightly

thickened. Remove the bowl from the heat.
4 Sprinkle the gelatin over the water in a heatproof bowl. Leave to soak 5 minutes until spongy, then stand the bowl in the pan of gently simmering water 1-2 minutes, stirring occasionally, until the gelatin has dissolved.
5 Beat the gelatin into the coconut cream mixture, together with the lime rind and most of the shredded coconut. Allow the mixture to cool about 30 minutes.
6 Meanwhile, secure a paper collar carefully around an 3¾-4 cup capacity soufflé dish.

7 In a spotlessly clean dry bowl, beat the egg whites until they stand in stiff peaks, then fold into the cooled coconut cream mixture. Transfer to the prepared soufflé dish and refrigerate at least 3 hours.
8 Meanwhile, brown the remaining shredded coconut: put the coconut on a foil-covered broiler pan and toast under a fairly hot broiler 2 minutes, turning constantly, until evenly browned.
9 Carefully remove the paper collar from the soufflé, then, using a spatula, press the toasted coconut onto the sides. Decorate the top with lime slices.

Cook's Notes

 TIME
Preparation takes 1 hour, plus 30 minutes cooling and at least 3 hours chilling.

BUYING GUIDE
If canned coconut cream is difficult to obtain, use 4½ oz block creamed coconut

dissolved in about 1 cup hot water.

 PREPARATION
Finely grate the rind from 1½ limes, then cut the remaining half into very thin slices for decorating.

● 680 calories per portion

FRENCH DINNER PARTY

Style and elegance are the hallmarks of French cookery, and here is a superb menu that captures these qualities. The three distinguished dishes include mouthwatering Garlic mushrooms, Dijon lamb noisettes in a gloriously creamy sauce and a fruity Currant sherbet — a selection of dishes that any French chef would be proud to serve. Bon appétit!

COUNTDOWN

The day before
- Make the Currant sherbet.

In the morning
- Prepare the Garlic mushrooms.

1 hour before
- Start the Dijon lamb noisettes.

40 minutes before
- Put the lamb dish in the oven.

20 minutes before
- Fry the Garlic mushrooms.

Just before the main course
- Remove the Currant sherbet from the refrigerator to soften.
- Make the mustard sauce, pour over the lamb and shallots.

Garlic mushrooms

SERVES 4

24 cup-shaped mushrooms (see Buying guide)
½ cup sweet butter, softened
2 cloves garlic, crushed
1 tablespoon finely chopped fresh tarragon, or 1½ teaspoons dried tarragon
finely grated rind of ½ lemon
freshly ground black pepper
2 eggs
¾ cup dried white bread crumbs
vegetable oil, for deep-frying
lemon wedges, to garnish

1 Carefully remove the mushroom stems and then chop up the stems finely.

2 Beat the butter with the mushroom stems, garlic, tarragon, lemon rind and pepper to taste, then spoon into the cavities of the mushroom caps. Sandwich the mushrooms together in pairs and secure with toothpicks.

3 Lightly beat the eggs in a bowl and spread the bread crumbs out on a plate. Dip each mushroom pair, first in the egg, then roll in the bread crumbs. Repeat once more, then refrigerate at least 1 hour.

4 Heat the oil in a deep-fat frier to 375° or until a stale bread cube browns in 50 seconds. Cook a few of the mushrooms about 5 minutes until golden brown. Drain on paper towels and keep hot in the oven while frying the rest.

5 To serve: Remove the toothpicks and serve at once.

Dijon lamb noisettes

SERVES 4

4 boneless lamb chops, each about 1½-inches thick
2 tablespoons vegetable oil
1 tablespoon butter
12 baby white onions
½ cup white wine
salt and freshly ground black pepper
bouquet garni
2 egg yolks
⅔ cup heavy cream
about 2 tablespoons Dijon-style mustard (see Buying guide)
1 bunch fresh herbs, to garnish (optional)

1 Preheat the oven to 375°.

2 Form the chops into neat rounds and secure with string.

3 Heat the oil and butter in a large skillet, add the lamb and cook briskly about 2 minutes on each side until browned. Transfer the lamb to a small roasting pan.

4 Add the onions to the fat remaining in the pan and cook gently 10 minutes until browned. Transfer to a lamb pan with a slotted spoon.

5 Pour the wine into the pan and bring to a boil, scraping up all the sediment from the base of the pan. Season to taste with salt and pepper, then pour over the lamb. Add the bouquet garni, cover with foil or a lid and bake in oven for 1 hour.

6 In a bowl, mix together the egg yolks, cream and 2 tablespoons of the mustard. Set aside.

7 Using a slotted spoon, transfer the cooked lamb and the onions to a serving dish and keep warm.

8 Discard the bouquet garni and strain the cooking liquid into a small, heavy-based saucepan. Boil briskly until the liquid is reduced by about half.

9 Pour a little of the hot cooking liquid into the egg yolk mixture, stirring vigorously all the time, then pour this mixture back into the pan. Heat through, stirring constantly, until thick and on the point of boiling. [!] Taste and adjust the seasoning, if necessary.

10 To serve: Pour over lamb and garnish with herbs, if liked.

Cook's Notes

Garlic mushrooms

TIME
About 45 minutes preparation, plus at least 1 hour chilling, then about 20 minutes cooking.

BUYING GUIDE
Buy the medium-sized cultivated mushrooms for this recipe, rather than the small or large, flat open varieties. The mushrooms must have cups deep enough to hold the filling.

- 380 calories per portion

Dijon lamb noisettes

TIME
Preparation takes about 30 minutes. Total cooking time is about 1 hour 10 minutes.

WATCHPOINT
Do not let the sauce boil or it may curdle and the mustard will turn bitter.

BUYING GUIDE
Dijon mustard, from the area of Burgundy south east of Paris, is available at most good supermarkets and specialty stores. Made from brown mustard seeds, it is a smooth mustard with a distinctive flavor. Dijon is also available with green peppercorns added — *moutarde au poivre vert*. Or, use a herb mustard based on Dijon mustard.

SERVING IDEAS
Serve with plainly boiled potatoes tossed in chopped parsley, if liked, plus broccoli or snow peas. For a really authentic flavor, serve a light, red French wine to complement the food — a Bordeaux wine (claret) would be the perfect choice.

If wished, follow the French custom of serving a tossed green salad or selection of cheese after the main course.

- 660 calories per portion

16

Currant sherbet

SERVES 4

½ lb fresh or frozen currants,
    without stems
½ cup sugar
1¼ cups water, plus
    2 tablespoons
2 teaspoons lemon juice
½ teaspoon unflavored gelatin
1 egg white

1 Put the sugar and the ½ cup water in a heavy-based pan and heat gently until the sugar has dissolved. Boil 10 minutes until syrupy, then remove from the heat and set aside to cool.

2 Put the currants in a pan with the lemon juice and heat gently about 10 minutes until softened. Allow to cool slightly, then purée in a blender. Press the puréed currants through a sieve into a bowl to remove seeds and skin.

3 Sprinkle the gelatin over the 2 tablespoons water in a heatproof bowl and leave to soak 5 minutes until spongy. Stand the bowl in a pan of gently simmering water and heat gently 1-2 minutes stirring occasionally until the gelatin has dissolved. Stir the gelatin into the cooled sugar syrup.

4 Stir the sugar syrup into the currant purée and mix well. Turn into a rigid container and freeze, uncovered, (see Cook's tip) about 3 hours until the mixture is firm around the edges.

5 Remove the currant mixture from the freezer and break up with a fork. Beat the egg white until it stands in stiff peaks, then fold into the currant mixture. ❄ Cover and freeze overnight, until solid.

6 To serve: Stand at room temperature about 30 minutes until the sherbet is soft enough to scoop into individual glasses.

SANGRIA EVENING

Conjure up an exotic, festive atmosphere at any time of year with a Sangria party. The delicious wine cup Sangria is a perfect accompaniment to food with a Spanish flavor – crunchy raw vegetables with a creamy dip. The Mediterranean Chicken catalan, and Spanish caramel custards with the sunny taste of orange.

To help create the informal atmosphere typical of a meal eaten in Spain, hand round the crudités before you and your guests sit down at the dinner table.

Sangria

SERVES 6
1½ quarts sweet red Spanish wine
5 fresh peaches, thinly sliced, or 1 can (about 14 oz) sliced peaches, drained
juice of 1 lemon
4 tablespoons brandy (optional)
1 dessert apple
1 lemon
2½ cups soda water
ice cubes

1 Put the peaches in a pitcher or glass bowl. Add the wine, lemon juice and brandy and allow to soak about 2 hours.
2 Just before serving, slice the apple and lemon thinly and add to pitcher with soda water and ice cubes.

Cook's Notes

TIME
10 minutes to prepare, but allow 2 hours for the full flavor to develop.

● 240 calories per portion

Crudités and dip

CRUDITES

SERVES 6
6 carrots
6 celery stalks
6 small or 3 large tomatoes
½ cucumber
8 radishes (optional)
1 small cauliflower

1 Top and tail, wash and pare the carrots. Cut into thin sticks.
2 Wash celery and cut into sticks.
3 Cut large tomatoes into quarters, leave small ones whole.
4 Cut the tails off the cucumber and pare it if you prefer. Divide into 2 both lengthwise and widthwise. Cut each piece into 4 long strips.
5 Wash, top and tail the radishes.
6 Wash, the cauliflower. Cut off the base then separate the head into flowerets. !
7 Arrange the crudités in groups around the edge of a tray, shallow basket or dish, leaving room for the dip in the center.

COTTAGE CHEESE AND YOGHURT DIP

SERVES 6
1 cup cottage cheese
2 tablespoons plain yogurt
2 scallions or ½ onion
1 dill pickle, finely chopped
salt and freshly ground black pepper
dash hot-pepper sauce (optional)

1 Strain or blend the cottage cheese until smooth.
2 Add the yogurt and mix well.
3 Wash and trim the scallions. Chop finely and add to mixture.
4 Add finely chopped pickle.
5 Season to taste and add hot-pepper sauce, if using.
6 Give a final mixing. Transfer to a serving bowl and place in center of crudités.

Cook's Notes

TIME
Allow 45 minutes to prepare the vegetables and make the dip.

COOK'S TIP
Save time by preparing the dip in a blender. Blend all the ingredients except the onions and pickles. Add these at the end and switch on for about 2 seconds so that they are only partially chopped.

● 40 calories per portion

WATCHPOINT
If vegetables are prepared in advance store them in a plastic box or in the salad drawer of the refrigerator to avoid wilting.

VARIATIONS
Use different varieties of vegetables such as red or green peppers, raw small mushrooms or small French beans.

● 45 calories per portion

Chicken catalan

SERVES 6

6 small chicken breasts, skinned
6 tablespoons olive oil
3 medium onions, thinly sliced
2 cloves garlic, crushed
2 cups long-grain rice
1-2 tablespoons tomato paste
pinch of saffron threads (see Steps)
   or few drops of yellow food
   coloring
5 cups boiling chicken broth
1 teaspoon paprika
salt and freshly ground black pepper
¼ lb Spanish chorizo sausage or
   other firm garlic sausage
   (optional), cut into large chunks
1 green pepper, seeded and sliced
   into rings
1 red pepper, seeded and sliced into
   rings
¾ cup stuffed olives
chopped parsley, to garnish

1 Heat half the oil in a large flame-proof casserole. Cook the chicken breasts over moderate heat until golden brown in color and half cooked through (about 7 minutes each side).

2 Reserve chicken pieces and keep them warm.

3 Add 1 tablespoon more oil to the casserole. Cook the onions over low heat 2 minutes until transparent but not brown.

4 Add the garlic, the remaining oil and the rice. Stir for a few minutes with a wooden spoon until the rice starts to color.

5 Meanwhile, stir the tomato paste and coloring, if used, into the boiling broth.

6 Stir broth, with saffron liquid, if used, into the rice mixture, add paprika and salt and pepper to taste, then bring to a boil, stirring constantly.

7 Add the chicken to the casserole with the sausage and peppers, pressing them all well down into the rice.

8 Lower the heat, cover and simmer about 30 minutes or until the rice is just tender, stirring occasionally with a wooden spoon. Be careful not to overcook the rice so that it becomes mushy.

9 Add the olives to the rice and heat through for a few minutes. Taste and adjust seasoning.

10 Transfer to a large warmed serving dish. Sprinkle the chopped parsley over the top to garnish and serve at once.

HOW TO USE SAFFRON

 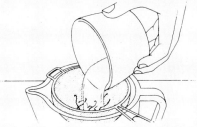 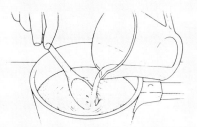

1 *Crush a few threads of saffron in your fingers and drop them into a small bowl of boiling water.*

2 *Leave to infuse at least 2 hours, then strain the water, discarding the saffron threads.*

3 *Stir the saffron-colored liquid into the broth used in recipe.*

Spanish caramel custards

SERVES 6

CUSTARD
- 1 orange
- 2½ cups milk
- 4 eggs
- ⅓ cup superfine sugar

CARAMEL
- 6 tablespoons granulated sugar
- 6 tablespoons water

1 Preheat the oven to 300°.
2 Wash and dry the orange, then pare off rind with a vegetable parer.
3 Place the orange rind and milk in a saucepan and allow to infuse over low heat. This means bringing the milk to a boil slowly and allowing it to stand 10 minutes.
4 Beat the eggs and sugar together in a bowl and strain over the milk. Beat lightly to mix.
5 Half fill a roasting pan with warm water and place in the oven.
6 To make the caramel: Put the sugar and water in a saucepan. Heat slowly until the sugar has dissolved, then boil steadily without stirring until the sugar turns a pale golden brown. [!]
7 Pour caramel into individual custard cups or a 6-inch diameter soufflé dish. Leave about 2 minutes to set.
8 Remove roasting pan from the oven.
9 Strain the egg and milk mixture onto the caramel in the dishes and place in the roasting pan. Replace in the oven and cook until the custard is set – about 40 minutes to an hour.
10 Cool at least 3 hours, then chill in the refrigerator.
11 Remove the pith from the orange with a sharp knife and divide the flesh into sections.
12 Turn the custards onto a plate and arrange the orange sections on top or around the plate.

Cook's Notes

TIME
The custards take about 30 minutes to prepare and 1 hour to cook. Remember to allow at least 4 hours afterwards for the custards to cool and for chilling.

COOK'S TIP
Always use a heavy-based saucepan for making caramel as it will give an even spread of heat and help prevent burning.

WATCHPOINT
Do not take your eyes off the caramel once it begins to turn brown as it burns very easily.

● 215 calories per portion

MEDITERRANEAN MEAL

Transport your guests to the sunny shores of the Mediterranean with this continental-style menu. Small onion tarts provide a tempting appetizer, before the magnificent Provençal fish stew. And, to finish, sophisticated fruit salad captures all the sunshine flavor of the meal.

Genoese onion tarts

SERVES 6

1 sheet (½ of 17 oz package) frozen puff pastry, thawed
1 can (2 oz) anchovy fillets (see Preparation)
12 black olives, halved and pitted

FILLING

1 lb onions, finely chopped
2 tablespoons butter or margarine
1 tablespoon olive oil
4 fatty bacon slices, chopped
1 teaspoon dried mixed herbs
½ teaspoon Dijon-style mustard
1 egg, beaten
2 tablespoons milk
salt and freshly ground black pepper

1 Make the filling: Heat the butter and oil in a skillet, add the bacon and cook over moderate heat 7-8 minutes. Remove the bacon from the pan with a slotted spoon and set aside. Remove the pan from heat and cool 10 minutes.
2 Add the onions to the fat remaining in the pan and cook very gently 15 minutes until they are soft and lightly colored.
3 Preheat the oven to 425°.
4 Meanwhile, dampen 6 individual 3-inch tart pans. Roll out the pastry very thinly on a lightly floured surface and cut out 6 rounds with a 3½ inch plain cookie cutter. Use to line tart pans and then prick base of each pie shell with a fork.
5 Add the herbs to the onions in the pan, together with the mustard, egg and milk. Mix well together, then season with salt and pepper.
6 Divide the filling between the tart shells, spread evenly and garnish with a cross made of anchovy strips and 4 olive halves.
7 Bake in the oven for about 25-30 minutes until the pastry is crisp and the filling is browned on top. Remove the tarts from the oven then carefully transfer them to a platter and serve while still warm.

Provençal fish stew

SERVES 6

2-2½ lb mixed fish fillets, skinned and cut into 2 inch pieces (see Buying guide)
6 tablespoons olive oil
2 large cloves garlic, crushed
1 sprig fresh fennel
bouquet garni
1-2 strips orange rind
1¼ cups dry white wine
salt and freshly ground black pepper
2 onions, thinly sliced
2 celery stalks, sliced
4 tomatoes, peeled, seeded and chopped
2 tablespoons tomato paste
5 cups fish broth or water
pinch of ground saffron (optional)
⅔ cup peeled shrimp, thawed if frozen
few cooked mussels, shelled
6 slices French bread, to serve
chopped parsley, to garnish

ROUILLE SAUCE

1 slice bread, crusts removed, soaked in water
1 chili, seeded and chopped
3 cloves garlic, crushed
1 egg yolk
⅔ cup olive oil

1 Place the fish in a large dish. Add 2 tablespoons olive oil, the garlic, fennel, bouquet garni and orange rind, then pour in the wine. Season well with salt and pepper, cover and leave to marinate at room temperature about 1 hour, stirring occasionally.
2 Heat 2 tablespoons of the olive oil in a large, heavy-based skillet or flameproof casserole, then add the onions and celery and cook gently 5 minutes until onions are soft and lightly colored then stir in the chopped tomatoes and the tomato paste and cook a further 2 minutes, stirring constantly with a wooden spoon.
3 Drain the fish and add the marinade to the pan. Stir in the fish broth and sprinkle in the ground saffron, if using. Bring to a boil, then simmer 20 minutes.
4 Meanwhile make the sauce: Squeeze the bread dry and put it into a bowl with the chili, garlic, egg yolk and a pinch of salt. Beat together with a little of the oil until well blended. Gradually beat in the remaining oil and season to taste with salt and pepper. Transfer the sauce to a serving bowl, cover with plastic wrap and set aside until it is required.
5 Discard the fennel, bouquet garni and orange rind from the drained fish, then add the marinated fish pieces and any remaining juices to the pan. Bring to a boil and then simmer, uncovered, about 15 minutes.
6 Add the shrimp and mussels. Simmer a further 5 minutes or until the fish is still in pieces but flakes easily when it is tested with a fork.
7 Meanwhile, cook the French bread in the remaining 2 tablespoons of oil until crisp.
8 To serve: Taste the stew and adjust seasoning, if necessary. Transfer to large, individual soup plates, sprinkle with parsley and serve at once. Serve the fried French bread and rouille sauce separately (see Serving ideas).

Cook's Notes

Riviera fruit salad

SERVES 6
2 cups heavy cream
4 teaspoons Strega liqueur (see Did you know and Variations)
1 cup strawberries
2 bananas
2 dessert apples
1 cup green grapes, halved and pitted

CARAMEL SAUCE
1 cup superfine sugar
8 tablespoons water

1 Make the caramel sauce: Put the superfine sugar in a heavy-based saucepan together with 2 table-spoons water. Heat very gently, until the sugar has dissolved. Bring to a boil and boil rapidly without stirring, until the syrup turns a rich caramel color. !

2 Remove from the heat and add the remaining water, 1 tablespoon at a time, taking care as it will splutter when the water is added to the very hot caramel. Stir well together, returning to the heat if necessary, until well blended. Set aside to cool about 2½ hours.

3 Beat the cream until standing in soft peaks, then fold in the liqueur (see Cook's tip). Divide between 6 individual shallow glass dishes, about 5 inches in diameter, and smooth over top with a knife. Cover and refrigerate at least 1-2 hours.

4 Just before serving, slice the strawberries, slice the bananas, then core and slice the apples. Arrange, with the grapes, in neat rows on top of the chilled cream and carefully coat with the caramel sauce. Serve the fruit salad at once.

Cook's Notes

TIME
45 minutes preparation, plus cooling the syrup and chilling the cream, then 10 minutes finishing the salad.

DID YOU KNOW
Strega is a sweet, citrus liqueur from Italy.

 VARIATIONS
Use different varieties of fruit or liqueur to taste — apricot- or cherry-flavored liqueurs are both suitable.

COOK'S TIP
Sugar is not added to the cream — the caramel sauce sweetens the dish.

WATCHPOINT
It is important not to stir the syrup while it is boiling as this may crystallize the sugar. Watch the caramel carefully — if it is too dark, it will taste strong and rather bitter.

● 525 calories per portion

NEW YEAR'S PARTY

Celebrate New Year's Eve with a flourish. Start the evening with drinks accompanied by Finnan haddie tarts, then launch into a full-flavored beef casserole. End the meal in spirited style with Drambuie creams.

Finnan haddie tarts

MAKES 24 TARTS

13 oz Pie Crust Sticks
1¼ lb finnan haddie
1 teaspoon ground mace
2 bay leaves, crumbled
freshly grated nutmeg
freshly ground black pepper
milk
2 tablespoons butter
1 tablespoon all-purpose flour
1 egg yolk, beaten
salt and freshly ground black
    pepper
pinch of cayenne pepper
grated Parmesan cheese

1 Preheat the oven to 375°.
2 Roll out the pastry on a lightly floured surface and cut out 24 circles with a 3-inch fluted cookie cutter. Use to line 24 tart pans and prick the base of each with a fork.
3 Line shells with foil and weight down with baking beans. Bake blind in the oven 10-15 minutes. Remove the foil and beans and set aside to cool.
4 Meanwhile, put the finnan haddie in a large saucepan with the mace, bay leaves, and a generous sprinkling of nutmeg and black pepper. Add enough milk to cover the fish, then poach gently about 15 minutes or until it flakes easily with a fork.
5 Using a slotted spoon, transfer the fish to a plate, then strain the cooking liquid. Make up the cooking liquid to 1¼ cups with milk and reserve.
6 Remove the skin and bones from the fish, then transfer to a bowl and mash extremely thoroughly with a fork.
7 Melt the butter in a small saucepan, sprinkle in the flour and stir over a low heat 1-2 minutes until

straw-colored. Remove from the heat and gradually stir in the reserved milky cooking liquid. Return to the heat and, stirring constantly, simmer until thick and smooth.
8 Add 1 beaten egg yolk and the mashed fish, stirring well to mix thoroughly. Taste and adjust seasoning, adding more salt, pepper and nutmeg if necessary.
9 Preheat the broiler to high. Carefully remove the tart shells from the pans, put on a large flameproof serving dish and divide the fish mixture between the shells. Sprinkle each one with a pinch of cayenne and a little Parmesan cheese.
10 Put under broiler 3-4 minutes until the cheese is melted and the tops of the tarts bubbly and golden. Serve at once.

Scotch beef casserole

SERVES 12

5 lb chuck steak, cut into 1 inch
    cubes (see Buying guide)
3 tablespoons olive oil
¼ cup butter
3 Bermuda onions, thinly sliced
2 tablespoons all-purpose flour
1½ lb tomatoes, peeled
2½ cups beef broth
salt and freshly ground black
    pepper
1 lb small mushrooms
1 tablespoon red currant jelly
2 teaspoons Dijon-style mustard

MARINADE

2½ cups medium red wine
3 tablespoons olive oil
3 cloves garlic, crushed
1 teaspoon juniper berries, crushed
3 bay leaves
2 sprigs fresh thyme, or ¾ teaspoon
    dried thyme
1 teaspoon ground caraway seeds

1 Mix the marinade ingredients together. Put the beef cubes in a large bowl and pour the marinade over them. Stir well to mix, then cover and marinate overnight.
2 Drain the meat, reserving the marinade. Remove the bay leaves and sprigs of thyme from the drained meat, then pat dry.
3 Heat the oil and butter in a large deep flameproof casserole. Add enough meat to cover the base of the pan and cook briskly 3-4 minutes until brown on all sides. Remove the meat with a slotted spoon, set aside. Cook remaining meat in batches.
4 Add the onions to the pan and cook gently 5 minutes until soft and lightly colored. Return the meat to the pan, sprinkle over the flour and cook, stirring, a further 5 minutes.
5 Add the tomatoes, broth and reserved marinade to the casserole with salt and pepper to taste. Bring to a boil, then lower the heat, cover and simmer 2-2½ hours.
6 Add the mushrooms to the casserole and simmer for 5 minutes.
7 Add the red currant jelly and mustard to the pan and simmer a further 10 minutes, stirring occasionally. Taste and adjust seasoning, if necessary. Serve hot.

COUNTDOWN
The day before
●Marinate meat for casserole.
In the morning
●Make and bake blind the tart shells for the Finnan haddie tarts.
●Toast the oatmeal for the creams.
3½ hours before
●Start cooking the casserole.
1 hour before
●Make the filling for the tarts.
30 minutes before
●Make the Drambuie creams.
15 minutes before
●Add mushrooms to casserole.
10 minutes before
●Complete the casserole.
●Fill the tarts and broil them.

Cook's Notes

Finnan haddie tarts

TIME
30 minutes preparation, 50 minutes cooking.

● 100 calories per tart

Scotch beef casserole

TIME
30 minutes preparation, plus 12 hours marinating, then 3-3½ hours cooking.

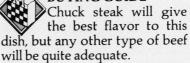
BUYING GUIDE
Chuck steak will give the best flavor to this dish, but any other type of beef will be quite adequate.

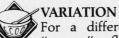
VARIATION
For a different, more "gamey", flavor, try using stewing venison. It is very rich so decrease the amount to 4½ lb.

SERVING IDEAS
Serve with generous helpings of mashed rutabagas mixed with mashed potatoes and butter and seasoned generously with freshly ground black pepper and salt — it is a delicious way to mop up the rich sauce of the casserole.

● 480 calories per portion

Drambuie creams

SERVES 12

4 cups heavy cream
½ cup fine oatmeal
½ cup confectioners' sugar
4 tablespoons Drambuie

1 Preheat broiler to moderate.
2 Spread the oatmeal out in a thin layer on a cookie sheet, and broil 3-4 minutes, turning once, until lightly toasted. Remove and leave to stand until completely cold.
3 Pour the cream into a large bowl and beat until it stands in soft peaks. ⚠
4 Add the cold oatmeal, sugar and Drambuie and stir until thoroughly mixed.
5 Spoon into individual glasses or custard cups and chill in the refrigerator 30 minutes before serving.

Cook's Notes

TIME
8-10 minutes preparation, plus, cooling time and 30 minutes chilling.

WATCHPOINT
Be careful not to beat the cream too stiffly otherwise the dessert may become too thick when the other ingredients are added.

DID YOU KNOW
This is an unusual adaptation of the famous Scottish drink Atholl Brose, which is made from Scotch whisky, cream and oatmeal.

Drambuie is a famous Scottish liqueur, based on the finest Scotch whisky. The name Drambuie is derived from the Gaelic *an dram buideach*: "the drink that satisfies". The secret recipe is alleged to have been give to the Mackinnon family by Bonnie Prince Charlie in return for saving his life.

● 365 calories per portion

VALENTINE'S DINNER

Valentine's day is traditionally a day for romance, so this year why not whet the appetite with a delicious dinner just for two. The dishes chosen — avocados, stuffed trout and a creamy heart-shaped dessert — have a seductive delicacy about them that sets the tone for a romantic and very intimate evening.

Avocado special

SERVES 2
1 large ripe avocado
juice of ½ lemon
¼ cup thick-type mayonnaise
1 slice cooked ham, finely chopped
1 tablespoon chopped chives
¼ teaspoon Dijon-style mustard
salt and freshly ground black
    pepper

TO GARNISH
lettuce leaves
tomato flesh, cut into heart shapes
    (see Preparation)

1 Cut the avocado in half lengthwise and remove the seed. Scoop out the flesh with a teaspoon, leaving a thin lining of flesh on the inside of the shells.
2 Put the flesh in a bowl, sprinkle over the lemon juice, then beat until smooth. Add the mayonnaise, ham, chives and mustard, mix well and season to taste with salt and pepper.
3 Pile the mixture back into the avocado shells.
4 Line 2 individual plates with lettuce leaves, and arrange the filled avocados on the lined plates. Garnish the avocados with the tomato shapes and serve at once.

Trout with mushroom stuffing

SERVES 2
2 fresh or frozen trout, each
    weighing about 1 lb (see
    Preparation)
⅓ cup butter
1 small onion, finely chopped
2 cups finely chopped mushrooms
juice of ½ lemon
1 tablespoon chopped fresh parsley
½ cup fresh white bread crumbs
salt and freshly ground black
    pepper

TO GARNISH
sliced stuffed olives
parsley sprigs
4 lemon wedges

1 Preheat the oven to 375°.
2 Melt 2 tablespoons of butter in a skillet, add the onion and cook gently for about 5 minutes until soft and lightly colored.
3 Add the mushrooms to the onion with the lemon juice and cook gently 5 minutes until the mushrooms are soft and all the liquid has evaporated.
4 Remove the pan from the heat and stir in the parsley and bread crumbs. Season to taste with salt and pepper and allow to cool.

5 Fill each trout with mushroom stuffing, then close openings with 2-3 wooden toothpicks.
6 Put the remaining butter into a shallow ovenproof dish large enough to hold the trout side-by-side. Place the dish in the oven for a few minutes until the butter melts. Remove from the oven.
7 Place the stuffed trout in the dish and turn them in the melted butter until they are well coated. Sprinkle with salt and pepper to taste.
8 Bake the trout, uncovered, 25-30 minutes until the flesh flakes easily when tested with a fork. Baste frequently during cooking.
9 Transfer trout to a hot serving plate, remove the toothpicks and garnish attractively with sliced olives and parsley sprigs. Serve at once, with lemon wedges.

COUNTDOWN
The day before
● Make the *Coeurs à la crème* and refrigerate overnight.
1¾ hours before
● Fill the Trout with mushroom stuffing and make the garnishes.
1 hour before
● Sprinkle the soft fruit with sugar for *Coeurs*.
30 minutes before
● Preheat oven and put in trout.
● Prepare the Avocado special.
Just before the dessert
● Unmold *Coeurs* and decorate.

Cook's Notes

Avocado special

TIME
This appetizer takes 20 minutes to make.

PREPARATION
Use a petits fours cutter to cut out hearts.

● 420 calories per portion

Trout with mushroom stuffing

TIME
About 30 minutes preparation, and 25-30 minutes cooking.

PREPARATION
Fresh trout should be gutted, rinsed under cold running water and patted

inside and out with paper towels. Your fishmonger will gut them for you, if asked.

SERVING IDEAS
Serve with sauté potatoes and tender, young peas (*petits pois*).

● 605 calories per portion

29

Coeurs à la crème

SERVES 2

½ cup cream cheese
1 tablespoon superfine sugar
finely grated rind of ½ lemon
⅔ cup heavy cream
1 egg white
2 cups fresh or frozen small
    strawberries or raspberries
extra superfine sugar

1 Line 2 *coeurs à la crème* molds (see Buying guide) with large squares of wet cheesecloth. ⚠ Allow the cheesecloth to hang over the sides.
2 Pass the cream cheese through a nylon sieve into a bowl, add the sugar and lemon rind and beat well until very soft.
3 Beat 4 tablespoons of the cream until it forms soft peaks, then mix into the cheese mixture.
4 Beat the egg white in a clean, dry bowl until it stands in stiff peaks. Fold 1 tablespoon of the egg white into the cheese mixture to lighten it, then fold in the rest.
5 Spoon the cheese mixture into the prepared molds and smooth the

tops. Fold the overhanging pieces of cheesecloth over the cheese mixture to enclose it completely. Put the molds on a flat plate and refrigerate them overnight.
6 About 1 hour before serving, sprinkle the strawberries with sugar to sweeten.
7 To serve: Remove the molds from the refrigerator and unwrap the

tops. Place a small serving plate on top of each mold, then carefully invert the plate and mold together. Shake gently, unmold, then carefully remove the cheesecloth.
8 Decorate with some of the fruit then pour over the remaining unwhipped cream. Put the remaining fruit in the empty molds and serve separately.

EASTER WEEKEND

Pretty, colorful eggs, whether to eat or to exchange, and the family gathering for a leisurely weekend meal, are what make Easter such an enjoyable occasion. Attractively marbled cooked eggs will make breakfast a special treat and the festively decorated eggs, which can be made in advance, may be passed round later on. For the main meal, a fruity appetizer, stuffed lamb and a triumphant meringue-topped dessert will appeal to both young and old. So start preparing for a wonderful Easter.

Marbled eggs

SERVES 6
6 large eggs
2 teaspoons each of green, red and
    blue food colorings (see
    Watchpoints)
12 slices white or brown bread,
    crusts removed
butter, for spreading
2-3 tablespoons sesame seeds

1 Preheat the broiler to high.
2 Put 2 eggs in each of 3 small saucepans and cover the eggs with water. Add 2 teaspoons of one of the food colorings to each pan and stir well. Bring the water to a boil and boil the eggs 2 minutes.
3 Meanwhile, toast the bread slices on one side only. Remove from the broiler and butter the untoasted sides, then sprinkle generously with sesame seeds. Set aside.
4 Remove the eggs from the water with a slotted spoon and, holding them in an oven glove, gently tap the shells all over with the back of a teaspoon, until they are cracked and crazed. [!]
5 Return the eggs to their pans, [!] bring back to a boil and boil for a further 1-2 minutes for soft eggs or 6-8 minutes for hard-cooked eggs.
6 Meanwhile, toast the sesame-coated sides of the bread until golden brown. Cut the toast into fingers or small points.
7 Drain the eggs and rinse under cold running water, then carefully remove the shells. Serve at once, with the sesame seed toast.

Chocolate eggs

MAKES 6
6 large eggs
24 squares (1½ lb) semisweet
    chocolate

DECORATIONS
a little lightly beaten egg white
about 1 cup confectioners' sugar,
    sifted
few drops of food coloring
sugar flowers or other
    decorations

1 Using a small skewer or a large darning needle, very carefully pierce a small hole in both ends of the eggshells. Enlarge one hole in each egg to about ¼ inch wide. Hold eggs over a bowl and blow out the contents through the larger of the holes.
2 Wash the eggs well in cold water, shaking out any remaining contents and put back in the egg box to drain and dry about 30 minutes.
3 Meanwhile, make a large and a small bag from greaseproof paper, without cutting off the ends.
4 When the eggshells are dry, place a small piece of sticky tape over each of the smaller holes.
5 Put the chocolate in a heatproof bowl over a pan of barely simmering water. Heat gently until melted, stirring occasionally, then pour into the large pastry bag.
6 Cut a small hole in the end of the bag and pipe the chocolate into the eggshells. Stand the eggs, sticky tape end downwards, back in the egg box. Allow the chocolate to settle for a few minutes, then top up with a little more chocolate, if necessary. Refrigerate the eggs in the box overnight until set.
7 When the eggs are set, crack them gently, then carefully peel off shells.
8 To decorate: Stand each egg in a glass. Add a little of the beaten egg white to the sugar and beat until the frosting forms stiff peaks, beating in more egg or sugar, if needed. Dot frosting onto the undersides of the decorations and fix in attractive designs to each egg (see Variations). Add a few drops of food coloring to remaining frosting, if liked, then use to fill the small pastry bag. Cut a small hole in the end and pipe leaves or other designs onto eggs.
9 Leave about 1 hour until set completely. Tie a small ribbon around each egg, fixing with a little frosting if necessary.

Cook's Notes

Marbled eggs

TIME
Preparing and cooking the eggs and toast take about 20 minutes.

WATCHPOINTS
It is very important to use only edible food colorings to tint the eggs.
    Tap the shells very gently to avoid damaging the eggs.
    Remember to put the eggs back in the same color water.

VARIATIONS
Try creating your own designs on shells of hard-cooked eggs. Use eggs with pale shells and draw or paint on patterns or face with felt-tip pens, water or oil paints.
    The eggs can also be boiled in food coloring to give color to the shell itself. To create patterns, cut out shapes from masking tape, stick them onto the eggs before boiling in colored water, then peel the tape away after boiling.

● 400 calories per serving

Chocolate eggs

TIME
Making the chocolate eggs takes about 40 minutes, plus setting overnight. Decorating the eggs takes about 30 minutes, plus setting time.

STORAGE
The decorated eggs can be made up to 1 week in advance, if stored in an airtight container in a cool dry place.

VARIATIONS
Here is a chance for the equipped cake decorator to be really creative. Use 2 cups confectioners' sugar and 1 large egg white to make frosting. Divide into bowls and add a few drops of food coloring to each. Using a petal tip, pipe your own flowers such as pretty daffodils onto waxed paper, then peel off and fix onto the eggs.

● 755 calories per serving

Melon and orange appetizers

SERVES 6
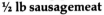

1 small honeydew melon
3 oranges
1 teaspoon chopped fresh mint,
    or ¼ teaspoon dried mint
2-3 teaspoons superfine sugar
6 mint sprigs or matchstick
    strips of blanched orange rind
    to garnish

1 Cut the melon in half and scoop out the pits. Cut the flesh into balls with a melon baller and put into a bowl, together with the melon juice (see Variations).

2 Squeeze the juice from half an orange and add to the melon balls. Pare the remaining half orange and the 2 whole oranges over a bowl to catch the juices. Use a fine serrated knife and a sawing action so that the rind is removed together with the pith. Section the oranges and discard the pits and membranes from between the sections.

3 Add the orange sections and juice to the melon with the mint. Sweeten to taste with sugar and mix lightly together.

4 Divide the melon and orange mixture between 6 individual glass dishes and garnish each portion with a sprig of mint.

5 Cover and refrigerate up to 1 hour before serving.

Lamb with walnut stuffing

SERVES 6
3-3½ lb leg of lamb, boned (see
    Buying guide)
½ lb sausagemeat
1 cup finely chopped shelled
    walnuts
2 tablespoons chopped fresh
    parsley
¼ teaspoon freshly grated nutmeg
1 teaspoon dried rosemary
salt and freshly ground black pepper
fresh parsley, to garnish

1 Preheat the oven to 400°.
2 Put the sausagemeat in a bowl together with the walnuts, parsley, nutmeg and half the rosemary. Season to taste and mix well.
3 Pack the stuffing into the boned cavity of the lamb, then secure with a trussing needle and fine string or meat skewers.
4 Place the lamb, fat side up, on a rack in a roasting pan and sprinkle with the remaining rosemary and salt and pepper to taste. Cover with foil. Roast in the oven 30 minutes, then lower the heat to 325° and roast a further 1½ hours. Remove the foil for the final 30 minutes of roasting.
5 Transfer to a serving platter, remove the string or skewers and serve, carved into slices and garnished with parsley.

Cook's Notes

Melon and orange appetizers

 TIME
Preparation time is about 15 minutes, chilling time 1 hour.

 VARIATIONS
Instead of cutting the melon flesh into balls, thickly pare off the rind and cut the melon into cubes.
    Use mandarins or satsumas in place of oranges – use 4 if they are small.
    Add 1 tablespoon toasted almonds for extra crunch.

● 55 calories per portion

Lamb with walnut stuffing

 TIME
30 minutes preparation, cooking 2 hours.

BUYING GUIDE
Ask your butcher to bone the leg of lamb: it is essential to order in advance, especially at Easter time.

 SERVING IDEAS
Serve with a selection of buttered carrots, turnips and new potatoes, and hand round mint jelly.

● 520 calories per portion

Princess dessert

SERVES 6

2 tablespoons butter
2 cups whole wheat bread crumbs
finely grated rind of ½ lemon
2 cups milk
3 eggs, separated
3 tablespoons black cherry jelly
scant 1 cup firmly packed light
   brown sugar

1 Preheat the oven to 325°. Generously grease a 1 quart ovenproof dish with butter.
2 Mix the bread crumbs with the lemon rind, milk and egg yolks. Pour into the greased dish and dot with the remaining butter.
3 Bake in the oven about 40 minutes or until the mixture is set. Remove from oven (see Cook's tip).
4 Put the jelly in a small saucepan, heat gently until melted, then drizzle over bread crumb mixture.
5 In clean, dry bowl, beat the egg whites until they stand in stiff peaks. Beat in the sugar, 1 tablespoon at a time, beating thoroughly after each addition. Pile on top of jelly and return to the oven about 20 minutes or until the surface of the meringue is crisp and lightly browned. Serve the pudding at once.

Cook's Notes

 TIME
Preparation 20 minutes, cooking 1 hour.

 SERVING IDEAS
Serve the dessert with light cream.

COOK'S TIP
For convenience, bake the bread crumb base before cooking the lamb. When the lamb is cooked, return the pudding to the oven with jelly and meringue topping and cook just 10 minutes. Turn off oven and finish cooking as the oven cools 30-40 minutes.

● 280 calories per portion

MIDSUMMER NIGHTS DINNER

Conjure up your own midsummer night's dream with an elegant dinner-party menu that takes full advantage of all that's fresh and good in summer. Glowing with soft summer colors, our heady meal starts with a delicate asparagus soup and is followed by a sumptuous vision of cucumbered salmon. Frosted fruit and rose petals provide a fantasy finish.

Chilled asparagus soup

SERVES 8
1 lb fresh asparagus, cut into 2-inch lengths (see Buying guide)
1 chicken bouillon cube
salt and freshly ground white pepper
½ cup light cream
juice of 2 limes

TO GARNISH
8 whole unpeeled shrimp
8 thin fresh slices of lime, cut through to the center
about 3 tablespoons light cream

1 Bring a large pan of cold water to a boil, add the asparagus pieces and cook about 15 minutes until soft. Remove the asparagus with a slotted spoon and put in the goblet of a blender.
2 Rapidly boil the liquid left in the pan 5 minutes, then measure out 5 cups. Add bouillon cube to the measured liquid and stir until dissolved. Leave the liquid to cool slightly.
3 Add a little of the broth to the asparagus in the blender and blend until smooth.
4 Pour the asparagus purée into a large bowl, gradually stir in the remaining broth and season to taste with salt and pepper. [!]
5 Stir in cream, blend thoroughly, then gradually add the lime juice. Cover the bowl of soup with plastic wrap and refrigerate 2 hours until well chilled.
6 To serve: Pour the soup into 8 chilled individual soup bowls and hook 1 shrimp and a lime slice over the side of each bowl. Swirl 1 teaspoon of cream into each bowl of soup, and serve at once.

Salmon with fennel mayonnaise

SERVES 8
4 lb fresh salmon, cleaned and trimmed with head and tail left on (see Buying guide)
1½ quarts water
¾ cup dry white wine
1 small onion, finely sliced
1 lemon slice
2 sprigs fresh fennel
1 parsley sprig
1 bay leaf
6 whole black peppercorns
generous pinch of salt

FENNEL MAYONNAISE
⅔ cup thick-type mayonnaise
4 tablespoons chopped fresh fennel
1 teaspoon Pernod (see Did you know)

TO GARNISH
1 slice stuffed olive (optional)
1 large unpeeled cucumber, thinly sliced
8 small lettuce leaves
finely chopped fresh fennel
sprigs fresh fennel

1 Pour the water and wine into a large saucepan, then add the onion, lemon slice, fennel, parsley, bay leaf, peppercorns and salt. Bring to boil, then lower heat and simmer 30 minutes. Cool then strain.
2 Put the salmon into a fish kettle or a large roasting pan and pour over the strained broth. Bring to boil, then turn to the lowest possible heat, cover and simmer gently 20 minutes until the fish flakes with a fork. Remove the pan from heat and leave fish, still covered, to cool in the liquid overnight.

3 Make the fennel mayonnaise: Put the mayonnaise in a bowl with the fennel and Pernod and mix well together. Cover and refrigerate.
4 When the fish is completely cold, dampen a sheet of waxed paper with water. Remove the fish carefully from the cooking liquid with 2 fish slices, then transfer to the dampened waxed paper.
5 Using the tip of a round-bladed knife, carefully peel off and discard the skin.
6 Roll the fish gently over and remove the skin from the other side, then gently scrape away any bones along sides of fish. Transfer fish to a long serving platter.
7 Garnish the salmon: Place the olive slice over the eye, if liked, then completely cover the side of the fish with cucumber slices (see Preparation). Arrange remaining thin cucumber slices around the edge. Arrange the lettuce along one edge of the salmon, and spoon the fennel mayonnaise into the center of each leaf. Sprinkle the mayonnaise with chopped fennel, then garnish the edge of the dish with fresh fennel sprigs.

COUNTDOWN
The day before
● Cook the salmon and leave to cool overnight.
● Prepare frosted grapes and rose petals and leave to set overnight.
2¾ hours before
● Make the chilled asparagus soup and refrigerate.
2 hours before
● Make the fennel mayonnaise. Skin the salmon and garnish.
● Frost the strawberries.
Just before the meal
● Pour the soup into individual soup bowls and garnish.
Just before the dessert
● Assemble the frosted fruit and rose petals on a dish.

Cook's Notes

Chilled asparagus soup

TIME
35 minutes to make, plus 2 hours chilling.

WATCHPOINT
The bouillon cube adds a certain amount of salt to the liquid so be careful when seasoning.

BUYING GUIDE
Buy the thin green asparagus for this soup or, if available, the kind sold as *sprue* — very thin stalks not regarded good enough for eating whole. They are just as delicious for soup — and much less expensive than the graded varieties of asparagus spears.

● 55 calories per portion

Salmon with fennel mayonnaise

TIME
1½ hours preparation, including cooking the salmon; then overnight cooling, plus 20 minutes finishing.

PREPARATION
Start arranging the cucumber slices at the tail end and overlap them so that they resemble fish scales.

BUYING GUIDE
Salmon usually weighs between 5 and 10 lb; it is often difficult to obtain a small salmon so be sure to order your salmon in advance to avoid disappointment. It is highly perishable, so use at once.

DID YOU KNOW
Pernod is a French aniseed-tasting drink and is available in miniature-sized bottles. When water is added to Pernod, it turns quite white and cloudy.

● 450 calories per portion

Frosted fruit and rose petals

SERVES 8

large pink rose petals (see Watchpoint)

2 egg whites

½ cup superfine sugar

32 green pitted grapes, separated into small bunches

16 whole fresh strawberries, stems still attached

1 Lightly beat the egg whites in a bowl and spread the sugar onto a flat plate.

2 Frost the rose petals: Holding each by tweezers, dip first into the egg white, then sprinkle with the sugar, to coat both sides thoroughly. Spread out in a single layer on a plate, and leave to dry overnight.

3 Frost the green grapes: Holding each fruit by its stem, dip first into lightly beaten egg white, then roll in the sugar. Place on a large flat plate, making sure they do not touch each other, and leave to dry overnight.

4 Two hours before serving, repeat process with the strawberries.

5 To serve: Pile the strawberries and grapes carefully into a pyramid on a flat dish, then arrange the rose petals on top.

HALLOWE'EN PARTY

The pumpkins, apples and jacket potatoes in this menu are all traditional Hallowe'en fare, which are sure to be popular with children and adults alike. To add to the fun there is for the adults a vivid witches' brew. For the kids, serve milk shakes.

Witches' brew

MAKES 30 GLASSES
2½ cups dry vermouth
⅔ cup lime cordial
⅔ cup crème de menthe
1½ quarts soda water
Angostura bitters, to taste
    (optional)
about 24 ice cubes
3 limes, thinly sliced

1 Crush the ice cubes (see Cook's tips) and place in a pitcher or punch bowl.
2 Stir in the vermouth, lime cordial and crème de menthe, then the soda water. Mix well and add Angostura bitters to taste, if liked.
3 Float slices of lime on top; serve.

Lamb and pumpkin casserole

SERVES 12
 3 lb boneless lamb, trimmed of fat and cut 1 inch cubes (see Buying guide)
2 lb pumpkin, pared and cut into ½ inch cubes
4 tablespoons vegetable oil
2 large onions, chopped
4 cloves garlic, crushed
1 can (about 14 oz) tomatoes
2½ cups beef broth
1 teaspoon dried oregano
salt
freshly ground black pepper
¾ lb chorizo sausages, sliced (see Buying guide)
2 cans (about 14 oz each) chick-peas
sprigs of parsley, to garnish

1 Heat the oil in a large flameproof casserole, add the lamb (in batches if necessary) and cook over brisk heat until evenly browned on all sides. Remove the casserole from the heat and transfer the browned meat with a slotted spoon to a large plate. Set aside.
2 Return casserole to the heat. Lower the heat, add the onions and garlic and cook gently 5 minutes until the onions are soft and lightly colored.
3 Add the tomatoes with their juice, the broth, oregano and salt and pepper to taste. Bring to a boil, return the meat with its juices to the casserole, then add the chorizos. Stir well, lower the heat slightly, then cover and simmer gently 30 minutes.
4 Add the pumpkin cubes to the casserole together with the chick-peas and their canned liquid. Cover, bring back to a boil, then reduce the heat slightly and simmer gently a further 30 minutes.
5 Skim off any excess fat from the surface and taste and adjust seasoning if necessary.
6 Garnish with sprigs of fresh parsley and serve at once, straight from the casserole.

West country potatoes

SERVES 12
12 even-sized potatoes, scrubbed
vegetable oil, for brushing
salt
½ lb herbed cheese (with chives and onion) (see Buying guide)

1 Preheat the oven to 425°.
2 Prick the potatoes well with a fork, then brush each one with a very little oil.
3 Sprinkle the potatoes with salt and place in the oven, directly on the shelves. Bake about 1 hour or until they feel soft in the center when pierced with a skewer.
4 Just before serving, cut the cheese into 24 thin slices. Make 2 slits in each potato and put a slice of cheese in each slit. Serve at once while the potatoes are still hot.

Cook's Notes

Witches' brew
 TIME
Preparation takes about 5 minutes.

 COOK'S TIPS
Crush the ice in a strong blender, or in a food processor. If you do not have either, place the ice in a strong polythene bag, squeeze out the air and tie firmly. Beat with a wooden mallet or rolling pin.

 VARIATION
Add a little green food coloring if you prefer a darker green drink.

● 35 calories per glass

Lamb and pumpkin casserole
 TIME
30 minutes preparation, 1 hour cooking.

 FREEZING
After adding the pumpkin and chick-peas, cook 15 minutes only. Cool quickly, lift off and discard any excess solidified fat, then pack into rigid container. Seal, label and freeze for up to 3 months. To serve: Thaw overnight in the refrigerator, then turn into a casserole and simmer about 20 minutes or until heated through.

 BUYING GUIDE
Frozen joints of boneless lamb, such as shoulder, can be found in most supermarkets.
Spanish chorizos are sold cooked and uncooked: either type can be used for this casserole, but the cooked type is the most commonly available. If you have difficulty buying chorizos, use kabanos or a similar type of strong-flavored sausage.

● 520 calories per portion

West Country potatoes
TIME
5 minutes preparation, 1 hour cooking.

 BUYING GUIDE
If you have difficulty in buying the cheese, use plain Cheddar and sprinkle with finely chopped chives or chopped onions.

● 245 calories per portion

Caramel-topped apples

SERVES 12
6 crisp dessert apples
2½ cups dairy sour cream
⅓ cup superfine sugar
finely grated rind and juice of 3 oranges
matchstick strips of orange rind, to decorate

CARAMEL CHIPS
½ cup granulated sugar
⅔ cup water
vegetable oil, for greasing

1 Make the caramel chips: Grease a cookie sheet and put the sugar and water into a small, heavy-based saucepan. Heat gently, without stirring, until the sugar has dissolved, then bring to a boil and boil 5 minutes, until the syrup turns a deep golden color. ⚠

2 Immediately remove from the heat and plunge the base of the pan into a bowl of iced water. ⚠ Leave for a few seconds until the sizzling stops, then remove pan from water.
3 Pour the syrup immediately onto the greased cookie sheet to make a thin layer. Allow it to become completely cold.
4 Meanwhile, pour dairy sour cream into a large bowl and stir in sugar. Add orange rind and juice.
5 Core and slice the apples, mix into sour cream, then turn into a large, shallow serving dish. Cover and refrigerate until ready to serve.
6 Crack the set caramel with a rolling pin to form fine chips and sprinkle over the apple mixture (see Cook's tip). Top with orange rind.

Cook's Notes

TIME
20 minutes preparation, plus setting time for the caramel.

WATCHPOINTS
Watch the syrup constantly and be sure to remove it from the heat immediately it turns a deep golden color.
Plunging the pan into cold water stops the cooking: take care that no water splashes into the syrup, otherwise it will split.

COOK'S TIP
Do not sprinkle the chips over the dessert until just before serving, otherwise the caramel will become soft and melt into the mixture.

STORAGE
The caramel chips will keep in a dry, airtight container for a day or two, but after that they will become sticky.

● 205 calories per portion.

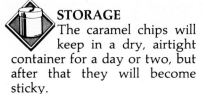

42

TEENAGE PARTY

The key to keeping a crowd of young teenagers happy is to provide heaps of hearty, unfussy food that they can tuck into with gusto. An authentic Italian lasagne, accompanied by garlic bread, is the perfect 'come-and-grab-it' style food. Served with an exciting-looking punch and rounded off with ice cream topped with hot sauces, this party is sure to be a winner!

Italian wine cup

MAKES ABOUT 60 GLASSES
About 2½ quarts Italian red wine
  (see Variations)
1 quart ginger ale
2 quarts lemonade or soda
  water
3 lemons, thinly sliced
2 oranges, thinly sliced
2 red-skinned apples
fresh mint sprigs
crushed ice

1 Put the wine, ginger ale and lemonade into a large bowl.
2 Add the sliced lemons and oranges. Leave the punch to stand 1 hour.
3 Just before serving, core and thinly slice the apples. Add to the punch with the mint sprigs and the crushed ice.
4 To serve: Ladle into pitchers together with some of the fruit, then pour into glasses.

Garlic bread

SERVES 10-12
3 long French loaves
1½ cups butter, softened
6 cloves garlic, crushed
4 tablespoons chopped parsley
  (optional)

1 Preheat the oven to 375°.
2 Beat the butter until creamy, then beat in the garlic and parsley, if using, until well mixed.
3 Cut each loaf diagonally into slices, about 2 inches thick, slicing to the base of the loaf but not cutting through it.
4 Spread the cut surfaces of the bread with the butter, then reform into a loaf shape. ✳ Wrap each loaf firmly in foil and place on a cookie sheet join side up.
5 Bake in the oven 15 minutes. Open the foil and bake a further 5 minutes to crisp the bread.
6 Remove the garlic bread from oven and serve it at once, straight from the foil.

Lasagne al forno

SERVES 10-12
1½ lb green lasagne (see Buying
  guide)
3 tablespoons olive oil
3 large onions, chopped
4 cloves garlic, chopped
3-3½ lb lean ground beef
2 cans (about 14 oz each) tomatoes
4 tablespoons tomato paste
1¼ cups Italian red wine
3 cups sliced mushrooms (optional)
2 teaspoons dried basil
salt and freshly ground black
  pepper
¾ cup grated Parmesan cheese
butter, for greasing

SAUCE
⅓ cup butter
¾ cup all-purpose flour
3¾ cups milk
freshly grated nutmeg

1 Heat the oil in large heavy-based skillet, add onions and garlic and cook gently 5 minutes.
2 Add the meat, turn the heat to high and fry until the meat is evenly browned, stirring with a wooden spoon to remove any lumps. Add the tomatoes with their juice, the tomato paste, wine, mushrooms, if using, basil and salt and pepper to taste. Bring to a boil, stirring well, cover and cook 30 minutes.
3 Preheat the oven to 375° and grease a rectangular ovenproof dish about 15 × 10 inches.
4 Make sauce: Melt butter in a pan, sprinkle in the flour and stir over low heat 1-2 minutes until straw-colored. Remove from the heat and gradually stir in all the milk. Return pan to the heat and simmer, stirring, until thick and smooth. Remove from the heat and season to taste with nutmeg, salt and pepper.
5 Spread one-third of the meat mixture in the bottom of the prepared dish. Place one-third of the lasagne on top in an overlapping layer, then spread over one-third of the white sauce. Repeat these layers twice more, ending with a layer of sauce.
6 Sprinkle with grated Parmesan cheese and bake in the oven about 45 minutes.

Hot-topped ice cream

SERVES 20
4 quarts vanilla ice cream

CHOCOLATE SAUCE
9 squares (9 oz) semisweet chocolate
¼ cup butter, softened
4 tablespoons milk
4 tablespoons clear honey
1 teaspoon vanilla

BUTTERSCOTCH SAUCE
¾ cup butter
1 cup firmly packed light brown sugar
2 tablespoons light corn syrup

RASPBERRY SAUCE
6 tablespoons raspberry jelly
juice of 1 lemon
2 teaspoons cornstarch
⅔ cup water
150 ml/¼ pint water

1 Make the chocolate sauce: Put the chocolate pieces in a small heavy-based saucepan. Beat in the butter, milk and honey and heat gently until the chocolate has melted. Add the vanilla (see Cook's tips).

2 Make the butterscotch sauce: Put all the ingredients in a heavy-based saucepan and heat gently until the sugar has dissolved. Bring to a boil and cook over high heat 3-4 minutes until the mixture is golden brown and thick (see Cook's tips).

3 Make the raspberry sauce: Put the jelly with the lemon juice in a heavy-based saucepan. Blend the cornstarch with 1 tablespoon of the water, then gradually stir in the remaining water. Stir into the jelly.

4 Heat gently until jelly has melted, bring to a boil and cook 2-3 minutes until the mixture is thick. Strain, return to the pan and heat through gently 2 minutes (see Cook's tips).

5 To serve: Pour the hot sauces into individual warmed pitchers; serve at once with the ice cream.

Cook's Notes

TIME
Each sauce takes about 10 minutes to prepare.

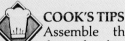
SERVING IDEAS
Serve the chocolate-topped ice cream with thin chocolate mints; serve the butterscotch-topped ice cream with chopped walnuts.

COOK'S TIPS
Assemble the ingredients for the chocolate and butterscotch sauces in advance, and place in pans ready for cooking when required. The raspberry sauce can be prepared in advance and reheated.

● 170 calories per portion ice cream. Plus 1 tablespoon chocolate sauce 90 calories; butterscotch 115 calories; raspberry 20 calories.

FAMILY PICNIC

A picnic by the sea is a great way to entertain the family, as long as the food is well planned. We have devised a picnic for six that can be made in advance and is easy to serve: we suggest a savory selection of pasties, ham rolls and chicken drumsticks, all of which are easy to eat with your fingers and can be neatly packed. The Banana creams for dessert are ready-made in sandproof containers, and are accompanied by crunchy shortbread fingers.

Tuna puff pasties

SERVES 6

2 cans (about 7 oz each) tuna, drained and flaked
1 tablespoon vegetable oil
1 onion, finely chopped
3 hard-cooked eggs, chopped
2 potatoes, boiled and diced
3 tablespoons tomato catsup
1 teaspoon dried mixed herbs
grated rind of 1 lemon
2 eggs, beaten
1 clove garlic (optional)
dash of Worcestershire sauce (optional)
salt and freshly ground black pepper
1½ sheets (¾ of 17 oz package) frozen puff pastry, thawed

1 Heat the oil in a skillet, add the onion and cook gently 5 minutes until soft and lightly colored. Transfer with a slotted spoon to a bowl.
2 Add the tuna to the bowl [!] together with the hard-cooked eggs, potatoes, tomato catsup, herbs, lemon rind, half the beaten egg, garlic and Worcestershire sauce, if using. Season with salt and pepper to taste and mix well.
3 Preheat the oven to 425°.
4 Roll out the pastry on a lightly floured surface: the larger sheet to an oblong 15 × 10 inches and the smaller sheet to an oblong 10 × 5 inches; cut into 6 × 7½-inch pieces.
5 Spoon a portion of the tuna and egg mixture onto the center of each piece of pastry. Brush the edges of each piece of pastry with water, then draw up the 2 long sides to meet over the filling. Firmly seal the edges together and crimp. Press the short sides together to seal them,

making a neat parcel. Repeat this process with the remaining pastry pieces.
6 Place the 6 parcels on a dampened cookie sheet and brush them with the remaining beaten egg. Bake in the oven 15-20 minutes until the pastry is golden brown and the underside is dry. Carefully transfer to a wire rack and leave to cool.

Herby chicken drumsticks

SERVES 6
6 chicken drumsticks
¾ cup dried white bread crumbs (see Preparation)
1 teaspoon dried rosemary
1 teaspoon dried thyme
1 teaspoon dried marjoram
salt and freshly ground black pepper
2 tablespoons all-purpose flour
2 eggs, beaten
2 tablespoons milk
2 tablespoons vegetable oil
¼ cup butter

1 Mix together the bread crumbs and herbs in a bowl and season well with salt and pepper. Place the flour in a plastic bag.
2 Put the beaten eggs in a shallow bowl and stir in the milk and a drop of oil. Put the bread crumb mixture on a plate. Shake each drumstick in the bag of flour to coat, then dip first into the egg mixture and then into the bread crumbs.
3 Heat the oil and butter in a large skillet over moderate heat. When the butter foams, add the drumsticks and cook gently about 20 minutes until cooked through and golden brown on all sides.
4 Remove the drumsticks, drain on paper towels and cool.

Ham rolls

SERVES 6

12 thin slices cooked ham
1 cup smooth liver pâté
3 tablespoons medium-dry sherry
2 tablespoons light cream
salt and freshly ground black pepper

1 Put the pâté in a bowl and mash it lightly with a fork.

2 Add the sherry and cream and mash well into the pâté until the mixture is smooth. Season with salt and pepper to taste.

3 Divide the mixture between the 12 slices of ham, spreading it evenly over each slice with a knife.

4 Carefully roll up each slice of ham as tightly as possible and secure with a toothpick.

Orange shortbread fingers

SERVES 6
1¼ cups all-purpose flour
⅓ cup ground rice
pinch of salt
½ cup butter, softened
¼ cup superfine sugar
grated rind of 1 small orange
butter, for greasing
superfine sugar, to decorate

1 Preheat the oven to 325° and lightly grease a cookie sheet.
2 Sift the flour, ground rice and salt onto a piece of waxed paper. Using a wooden spoon, beat the butter in a bowl until creamy, then beat in the sugar and orange rind until thoroughly combined.
3 Gradually work the sifted flour mixture into the butter mixture, using a wooden spoon at first and finishing by gathering the dough into a ball with your hands. [!]
4 Roll the dough out on a floured surface to an 8-inch square about ½-inch thick, patting the shortbread into shape with your fingers to give a neat edge.
5 With a fish slice, carefully lift the shortbread onto the greased cookie sheet and prick all over with a fork.

Bake in the oven 25 minutes until lightly colored. Immediately cut in half lengthwise, then cut into fingers.
6 Cool for 10 minutes on the cookie sheet until firm, then transfer to a wire rack to cool completely. Sprinkle with superfine sugar if wished.

Banana creams

SERVES 6
4 bananas
1 can (about 2 cups) evaporated milk
2 teaspoons sugar
juice of 1 lemon

1 Slice 3 bananas and put in a blender with the evaporated milk, sugar and lemon juice. Blend until thick and smooth. Alternatively, mash the sliced bananas with a fork until they form a smooth pulp, then beat in the remaining ingredients.
2 Divide the banana cream among 6 plastic containers (see Serving ideas) and refrigerate.
3 Just before serving, cut the remaining banana into diagonal slices and arrange on top of each portion. Serve the creams in the plastic containers.

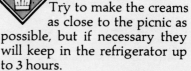

CHILDREN'S BIRTHDAY PARTY

Give a children's fancy-dress birthday party with an "animal" theme. Animal-shaped cheese crackers are good fun, and for those who like savories there are also sausages and bacon rolls stuck into a 'caterpillar' made from a cucumber. For an impressive centerpiece make our colorful butterfly cake, decorated with feather frosting.

The day before
- Make the animal crackers.
- Make the cake.

On the day
In the morning:
- Assemble and frost cake.

2 hours before
- Decorate the cake with sugar-coated chocolate buttons and add the liquorice "antennae".

1 hour before
- Prepare the cucumber and begin to cook the sausages and bacon and pineapple rolls.

Cucumber caterpillar

SERVES 12
1 large cucumber, preferably slightly curved
2 candied cherries
1 lb cocktail sausages (see Cook's tips)
6 slices fatty bacon, cut in half crosswise
1 can (about 8 oz) pineapple pieces, drained

1 Cutting at a slant, slice off the thicker end of the cucumber. To make the eyes: Spear each cherry on to the end of half a toothpick; press sticks in cut end of cucumber.
2 At the other end, with a sharp knife, make a few small cuts across the cucumber, about ⅛ inch apart, for the "tail".
3 Preheat the broiler to high.
4 Prick the sausages with a fork and cook over gentle heat until they are golden brown on all sides.
5 Meanwhile, wrap each half bacon slice around a piece of pineapple and secure with a wooden toothpick. Broil the bacon and pineapple rolls 3-4 minutes until the bacon is crisp. Drain on paper towels.

6 Drain the sausages and spear a toothpick into each one. Stick the sausages in a ridge down the center of the cucumber and the bacon rolls on either side and serve at once (see Cook's tips).

Animal cheese crackers

MAKES 50
2 cups all-purpose flour
pinch of salt
¼ teaspoon dry mustard
½ cup butter or margarine
¾ cup finely grated sharp Cheddar cheese, (see Watchpoint)
1 egg yolk
2 tablespoons water
little milk, for glazing
sesame seeds and/or poppy seeds
butter, for greasing

1 Sift the flour, salt and mustard powder into a large bowl. Rub in the butter until mixture resembles fine bread crumbs, then add the cheese. Mix in the egg yolk and water with a knife, then gather up the pastry in your hands to make a firm dough.
2 Turn the dough onto a lightly floured surface and knead briefly until smooth. Place in a plastic bag and leave to rest in the refrigerator 30 minutes.
3 Heat the oven to 400° and grease 2 cookie sheets.
4 Roll out the pastry on a floured surface until it is about ⅛ inch thick. Using different-shaped animal cookie cutters, cut out shapes and place on the greased cookie sheets spacing them apart to allow for them spreading during baking. Brush all over with milk. Using a skewer or point of a knife, make holes for the eyes, mouths, noses, etc.
5 Decorate the crackers with sesame seeds and/or poppy seeds.
6 Bake in the oven, in 2 batches 15-20 minutes each until golden brown. Remove from the oven, allow to settle 1-2 minutes, then place on a wire rack and leave to cool before serving.

Cook's Notes

Cucumber caterpillar

 TIME
Preparation time is about 30 minutes, cooking time about 10 minutes.

COOK'S TIPS
If you have difficulty buying cocktail sausages, buy thin ones and cut each in half by twisting skin in the middle then cutting it.
If you wish, keep the cucumber warm for 30 minutes in a 225° oven.

- 180 calories per portion

Animal cheese crackers

 TIME
30 minutes preparation, 30-40 minutes cooking, plus resting and cooling time.

 WATCHPOINT
Use a sharp Cheddar cheese or the crackers will lack flavor.

 STORAGE
These crackers will keep for 1 week in an airtight container in a cool, dry place.

- 35 calories per cracker

Butterfly birthday cake

MAKES 24 SLICES
2 cups self-rising flour
2 teaspoons baking powder
1 cup soft butter
1 cup superfine sugar
grated rind of 2 oranges
4 large eggs
butter, for greasing

FILLING AND DECORATION
¾ cup apricot jelly
½ cup flaked coconut
2 cups confectioners' sugar
2-3 tablespoons water
brown food coloring

TO FINISH
12-inch square of heavy cardboard,
    covered in foil
3 chocolate flake bars
candles and candle-holders
3 small packages of sugar-coated
    chocolate buttons
2 liquorice ropes

1 Preheat oven to 325°. Grease a deep 9-inch square cake pan. Line the sides and base of the pan with waxed paper, then grease.
2 Sift the flour and baking powder into a large bowl. Add the butter, sugar, orange rind and eggs. Mix well, then beat with a wooden spoon 2-3 minutes, or with a hand-held electric beater 1 minute, until blended and glossy.
3 Turn the mixture into the prepared pan and level the surface, then make a slight hollow in the center. Bake in the oven about 65 minutes, until the top of the cake is golden and springy to the touch.

4 Cool the cake in the pan for 5 minutes, then turn out onto a wire rack and peel off the lining paper. Leave the cake upside down to cool completely.
5 Trim the cake to level it off, if necessary. Slice the cold cake in half horizontally and sandwich together with 5 tablespoons of the apricot jelly. Cut the cake in half diagonally to make 2 triangles, then trim off the triangle tips opposite the cut edge.

6 Strain all but 1 tablespoon of the remaining jelly into a small, heavy-based saucepan and stir over low heat until melted. Brush the sides of the cakes, except the trimmed corners, with some melted jelly.
7 Spread a thick layer of coconut on a large plate. Press jelly coated sides of cake into the coconut one at a time until evenly coated. (Add more coconut to plate if needed.)
8 Brush the trimmed corner of each cake with melted jelly. Place the 2 pieces of cake on the cake-board, with the trimmed corners almost touching to make a butterfly shape. Place the chocolate flakes in the gap, one on top of another, then push the 2 "wings" together.
9 Make the frosting (see Cook's tips): Sift the sugar into a bowl, then beat in enough water to give a thick coating consistency.

10 Put 2 tablespoons of frosting into a small bowl. Add several drops of brown food coloring, mix well, to make a fairly dark frosting. Spoon frosting into a small pastry bag fitted with a writing tip.
11 Brush the top of the cakes with remaining melted jelly. Spread the white frosting smoothly and evenly over the top with a knife. Immediately ⚠️ pipe parallel lines of brown frosting down the "wings."

12 Draw a skewer through the brown lines to give a "feather" effect.

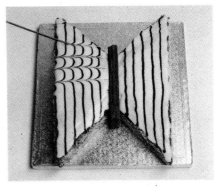

13 Neaten edges, removing surplus frosting; arrange the candles in their holders on top. Leave to set.
14 Two hours before the party, melt the remaining tablespoon jelly. Brush jelly on each chocolate button and stick them round the edges of the cake. Stick in 2 pieces of liquorice for the "antennae" and curl them round slightly.

Cook's Notes

TIME
20 minutes preparation, 65 minutes baking, plus cooling time. Shaping and decorating take about 1 hour.

COOK'S TIPS
Very fresh cake is difficult to cut and frost neatly, so bake the cake a day before decorating.

You can assemble and frost cake on the evening before the party, but not before, otherwise frosting will dry out and crack.

! **WATCHPOINT**
Speed is essential: the frosting must not start to set before "feathering".

● 265 calories per slice.

BURGER AND PIZZA PARTY

Create a relaxed atmosphere for family and friends, and cater for all ages from 4 to 50 plus, with a burger and pizza party. Featuring food that is both popular and easy to make, the menu also includes an unusual chocolate fondue which will add to the fun and informality. For outsize appetites you can double up on the quantities given here.

THE DAY BEFORE
● Make the tomato sauce for the pizzas, cover and refrigerate.
● Make the pizza dough and put into refrigerator to rise slowly overnight.
● Prepare and shape the burgers. Cover and refrigerate.
● Make the syrup for the fruit cup.
● Wash salad ingredients, wrap and refrigerate; make salad dressings and store in the refrigerator.

ON THE DAY
● Prepare ingredients for the pizza toppings and cake for the fondue.

JUST BEFORE THE PARTY
Remove pizza dough from the refrigerator, allow it to return to room temperature then knead again.
● Assemble the salads, but do not dress them.
● Prepare the fruit dips and the chocolate for the fondue.

PARTY TIME
● Finish making the fruit cup.
● Cook and serve the burgers.
● Complete and bake the pizzas.
● Dress the salads.

Beefburgers

MAKES 12 BURGERS
 1½ lb chuck steak (see Buying guide)
 1 large onion
2 cups fresh bread crumbs
salt and freshly ground black pepper
1 egg, beaten
2 tablespoons beef broth or water

TO SERVE
6 tablespoons vegetable oil
6 onions, sliced
12 burger buns
1 Bibb lettuce, separated into leaves
tomato slices

1 To make the burgers: Grind the meat finely by passing it through the mincer twice. Grind the onion.
2 Put the ground meat, onion and bread crumbs into a bowl and season with salt and pepper. Add the egg and broth and mix together with your hands until combined.
3 Divide the mixture into 12. On a floured board, shape each piece into a neat, flat 4-inch circle.
4 Line a cookie sheet or tray with plastic wrap, place the shaped burgers on top, then cover with plastic wrap. Refrigerate until required.
5 To serve: Heat 2 tablespoons oil in a large skillet, add the onion slices and fry gently until soft and lightly browned. Removed with a slotted spoon and drain on paper towels.
6 Preheat the oven to 250° then put the burger buns in the oven to warm while cooking the burgers. Keep the fried onions warm in the oven at the same time.
7 Heat 2 tablespoons oil in each of 2 large skillets. Put 6 burgers in each pan and cook gently about 5 minutes on each side, or until lightly browned and cooked.
8 Cut open the warm burger buns and fill each with a lettuce leaf, a burger, a slice of tomato and some fried onions. Serve at once.

Cook's Notes

TIME
Preparation 45 minutes, cooking 10-15 minutes.

BUYING GUIDE
Alternatively, buy best-quality ground beef for the burgers, although the burger will have more flavor if you grind your own beef.

FREEZING
Open freeze, pack in a plastic bag, seal, label and freeze. Store up to 2 months. To serve: Cook from frozen as in recipe.

SERVING IDEAS
Wrap each cooked burger in a paper napkin. Serve with a selection of pickles, relishes, and mustards.

● 305 calories per portion

Lemon and apple cup

MAKES ABOUT 2 QUARTS

thinly pared rind and strained juice
   of 2 lemons
1¼ cups sugar
2½ cups cold water
1 red skinned dessert apple
1 orange
1 lemon
1 quart apple juice or white wine,
   chilled (see Cook's tip)
2½ cups fizzy lemonade,
   chilled
mint leaves, to serve (optional)

1 Put the lemon rind and sugar into
a saucepan with the water. Heat
gently until sugar has dissolved,
then bring to a boil and boil 3
minutes. Remove from the heat,
cover and leave to stand at least 3
hours, preferably overnight.
2 Just before serving, strain the
lemon syrup into a chilled serving
bowl. Stir in the lemon juice.

3 Quarter and core the apple, but
do not pare, then slice it thinly and
add to the lemon syrup. Thinly slice
the orange and lemon (including the
rind) and add to the syrup. Pour the
apple juice and lemonade into the
bowl and stir well. Decorate with
mint leaves if liked; serve at once.

Cook's Notes

 TIME
Preparation time 15
minutes, cooking time
5 minutes, but allow at least 3
hours standing time for the
flavor of the lemon syrup to
develop.

 VARIATION
If fresh mint is out of
season, soak 1 teaspoon
dried mint in boiling water,
drain and add to the cup before
serving.

COOK'S TIP
Choose apple juice or
white wine for the cup
according to the age and
preferences of your guests.

● 145 calories per serving

Party pizzas

SERVES 12

PIZZA DOUGH
4 cups all-purpose flour
1 teaspoon salt
¼ cup butter or margarine
1 package active dried yeast
1 teaspoon sugar
1¼ cups tepid water
vegetable oil, for brushing and
    drizzling

TOMATO SAUCE
2 tablespoons olive or
    vegetable oil
3 medium onions, finely chopped
1 can (about 1¾ lb) tomatoes
2 tablespoons tomato paste
1 tablespoon dried mixed herbs
2 beef bouillon cubes
salt and freshly ground black pepper

TOPPINGS
¾ lb mozzarella cheese, thinly
    sliced
¼ lb thinly sliced salami, rinds
    removed, cut into strips
¼ lb cooked ham, cut into strips
1 cup thinly sliced small
    mushrooms
1 red pepper, seeded and thinly
    sliced
1 green pepper, seeded and thinly
    sliced
4 teaspoons capers
1 large onion, chopped
    (optional)
2 cans (about 2 oz each) anchovy
    fillets, drained
24 black olives

1 First make the tomato sauce: Heat the oil in a large saucepan. Add the onions and cook gently 5 minutes or until soft but not colored. Stir in the tomatoes with their juice, the tomato paste and the herbs. Crumble in bouillon cubes. Break up the tomatoes with a wooden spoon, then add salt and pepper to taste. Bring to a boil, stirring all the time. Reduce the heat to low, partially cover the pan and simmer about 1 hour. Cool.
2 Next make the pizza dough (see Cook's tips): Mix the yeast and sugar in a bowl and then add ¼ cup of tepid water. Leave for 10 minutes

until frothy. Sift flour and salt into a large bowl. Rub in the butter then make a well in the center of the flour and stir in the yeast mixture and the tepid water. Mix the ingredients together thoroughly to form a stiff dough.
3 Turn the dough onto a very lightly floured surface, then knead 10 minutes until smooth and elastic. Alternatively, knead it in an electric mixer, using a dough hook, 3 minutes. Put the dough back into the bowl, cover with plastic wrap or a clean dish towel and leave in a warm place for about 1 hour or until the dough has more than doubled in size.

4 Preheat oven to 400°. Lightly brush two 12-inch round ovenproof plates or two 14 × 12 inch oblong cookie sheets with vegetable oil (see Cook's tips).
5 Turn the risen dough onto a lightly floured surface, punch down then knead for a minute. Cut dough in half and form each half into a ball. Coat with oiled plastic wrap and leave to stand for 10 minutes.
6 Roll each piece of dough out to a round or an oblong to fit the prepared plates or cookie sheets. Place dough in position and press out firmly until it fits neatly. Finally carefully pinch up the edge of dough to make a neat raised rim.

7 Brush the dough with a little more oil, then spread with tomato sauce. Cover with the cheese to within ¼-inch from the edge. Arrange the salami, ham, mushrooms, peppers, capers, onion, if using, on top, in separate sections or mixed together (see Serving ideas). Divide off the sections with anchovy fillets and place black olives in each section. ✳

8 Drizzle a little oil over the surface, then bake in the oven about 25 minutes, or until the cheese is bubbling and golden. Cut the pizza into sections and serve at once accompanied by a varied selection of salads.

Cook's Notes

 TIME
Preparation time is 1½ hours, including rising time. Cooking time is about 25 minutes.

COOK'S TIPS
To save time you can use three packages ready pizza dough mix to make the pizza base. Cook according to package directions.

Choose cookie sheets with sides to contain the pizza dough neatly and stop it spreading.

 SERVING IDEAS
Invite party guests into the kitchen to select their own toppings which can be arranged in separate sections.

FREEZING
Open freeze after stage 7, seal in plastic bags, label and freeze. Store up to 3 months. To serve: Cook from frozen at 425° about 30 minutes.

● 375 calories per portion

Chocolate fondue

SERVES 12
14 squares (14 oz) semisweet chocolate, broken into small pieces
1¼ cups heavy cream
6 tablespoons sweet sherry
¼ cup sweet butter

DIPPERS
2 × 8-inch sponge cake layers
apricot jelly, for spreading
4 large bananas
2 tablespoons lemon juice
2 large dessert apples
1 can (about 1 lb) sliced peaches in syrup, well drained

1 First prepare the dippers: Slice the cake in half horizontally and sandwich with apricot jelly. Cut into neat 1-inch cubes. Peel the bananas, cut into slices ½-inch thick and toss in 1 tablespoon lemon juice. Quarter, core and slice the apples and toss in the remaining lemon juice. Leave peach slices whole, or cut into chunks if large. [!]

2 Arrange in separate bowls.

3 Put the chocolate into a heavy-based fondue pan or small saucepan and add the cream and sherry.

4 Just before serving, gently heat the chocolate, cream and sherry together until the chocolate melts, stirring all the time. Continue until almost, but not quite boiling. [!] Stir in the butter until melted.

5 Place the pan over a small spirit burner on the table. Arrange the bowls of cake and fruit around the fondue, along with fondue or ordinary forks for spearing the cake and fruit before they are dipped in.

SUNDAY LUNCH FOR SIX

Sunday lunch is traditionally a time when the whole family sits down for a meal together. Even if you have little time for cooking during the week, it is worth treating Sunday lunch as a special occasion and making an extra effort, particularly if you have guests as well as the family.

If you have any spare time, you can begin the preparations the day before, to ease your workload next morning. Use the countdown below to help you time both cooking operations and the serving of the meal to perfection.

The day before
Thaw the puff pastry overnight so that you can make the dumplings in the morning.
Thaw the shrimp overnight if using frozen.

On Sunday morning
Make the grapefruit cocktails and then refrigerate.

Pare the potatoes and keep them in water to prevent browning. Pare the apples and onion. Keep the apples in salted water to prevent browning and wrap onion in plastic wrap. Prepare the other vegetables you have chosen for the meal.
11.00 Prepare the pork for cooking in its roasting pan and put in the oven for the time required.
11.45 Prepare the fruit filling and roll out and cut the pastry. Make the dumplings and put on a cookie sheet.
12.10 Drain the potatoes, dry them with a clean cloth and coat in oil. Slice the onion and apples, place them around the pork and put the potatoes on top. Pour over the apple juice and return the roasting pan to the oven (see Recipe).
12.30 Cook the other vegetables. Make gravy in your usual way (you can also use the thin cooking juices under the pork). Drain vegetables when they are ready and put them in warm serving dishes. Cover and keep hot.
1.00 Serve the first course.
1.15 or 1.30 Reduce oven and bake the dumplings.

Grapefruit and shrimp cocktail

SERVES 6
3 small grapefruit
1 cup peeled shrimp
1 tablespoon chopped parsley
5 tablespoons mayonnaise
salt
pinch of cayenne pepper (optional)
3 lettuce leaves, finely shredded
1 teaspoon ground ginger (optional)
parsley to garnish

1 Halve the grapefruit, vandyking the edges: To do this use a sharp knife to cut V-shapes all round, cutting right through to the center of the grapefruit. Separate the halves and remove the flesh, discarding all the white pith. Reserve the shells.
2 Separate the grapefruit flesh from the pith and the membranes.
3 Drain the grapefruit flesh and

shrimp well, then mix them with the parsley and mayonnaise. Add salt and cayenne pepper to taste.
4 Line each reserved grapefruit shell with lettuce, then divide the shrimp mixture equally between them and place each on a small plate.
5 Cover and chill at least 30 minutes before serving.
6 Sprinkle on ground ginger, if using, and garnish with parsley.

Cook's Notes

TIME
Preparation time 20 minutes. Allow at least 30 minutes chilling time.

COOK'S TIP
Use a good commercial mayonnaise — a home-made one may separate.

● 120 calories per portion

Apple roast pork

SERVES 6

3 lb boneless pork joint
salt
3 tablespoons vegetable oil
2 sprigs fresh rosemary, or 2
   teaspoons dried rosemary
3 lb potatoes, thickly cut
2 dessert apples
1 medium onion, thinly sliced
¾ cup apple juice
freshly ground black pepper

1 Preheat the oven to 350°. Weigh the joint of pork and calculate the exact cooking time, allowing 25 minutes per 1 lb plus an extra 25 minutes.

2 Check that the butcher has scored the skin of the pork to make crackling. If he has not, do this yourself with a sharp knife (see Preparation).

3 Wipe the pork dry. Sprinkle the skin with salt and rub it lightly with ½ tablespoon oil.

4 Put the rosemary sprigs in a roasting pan or sprinkle in the dried herbs. Place the pork on top.

5 Roast the joint in the oven about 1¾ hours, or according to the calculated cooking time per weight.

6 About 1¼ hours before the end of the cooking time, put the potatoes in a bowl with the remaining oil and shake well to coat. Pare, core and slice the apples.

7 Remove the pork from the oven, scatter the apple and onion around the joint, then place the potato pieces on top of them. Pour in the apple juice. Sprinkle with salt and pepper.

8 Return the pan to the oven and continue roasting a further 30 minutes.

9 Turn up the oven to 500°, and then cook a further 30 minutes. The pork crackling should be crisp and the potatoes golden.

10 Place the pork on a warmed carving dish and arrange the apple, onion and potato around the pork or, for easier carving, in a separate dish. Serve at once.

Cook's Notes

TIME
Preparation time is 5 minutes. Exact cooking time will depend on the size of the joint, but will be approximately 1¾ hours for the weight recommended here.

If the meat is cooked before you are ready, turn down the oven and keep the roast warm.

SERVING IDEAS
Shredded red cabbage baked in the oven with sliced cooking apple, onion, chicken broth and a dash of vinegar is a good sharp accompaniment to the richness of the roast pork and crackling.

Serve dry white wine as a drink with the meal to complement the flavors of the food.

PREPARATION
Scoring pork: Using a very sharp knife, make parallel cuts in the pork skin about ½-inch apart. Make sure that you cut right through the skin, to the thin layer of fat beneath the skin.

Crush dried rosemary well, to avoid any sharp spikes.

● 1110 calories per portion

Appleberry dumplings

SERVES 6

6 dessert apples
1 can (about 1 lb) blackberries,
    drained
juice of ½ lemon
1 package (17 oz) frozen puff pastry,
    thawed
1 large egg, beaten
superfine sugar
cream to serve (optional)

1 Preheat the oven to 425°.
2 Pare the apples and core carefully with an apple corer or vegetable parer. Brush with lemon juice.
3 Roll out the pastry on a lightly floured surface and trim to a 12 × 8 inch rectangle, then cut into 6 squares.
4 Pat the apples dry with paper towels. Place an apple on each square of pastry, then divide the drained blackberries equally between the apples, pressing them into the apple cavities.
5 Brush the pastry edges with some of the beaten egg, then wrap each apple loosely but completely sealing the joins firmly. !
6 Place the dumplings, seam-side down on a dampened cookie sheet. Roll out the pastry trimmings and use to make leaves. Brush with cold water and place on top of the dumplings. Brush each one with the remaining egg and sprinkle with the sugar. ! Make a small hole in the top of each dumpling to allow steam to escape during baking.
7 Bake in the oven 15 minutes then reduce to 350° and cook for a further 10 minutes until the apples are tender when pierced with a skewer. Serve with cream.

Cook's Notes

TIME
Preparation and cooking can be completed in 50 minutes.

VARIATIONS
When in season, use fresh blackberries. Also try using blackberry jelly.

WATCHPOINT
While cooking, the apples expand. It is therefore essential to wrap them *loosely* in the pastry or it will break open.

To help prevent the pastry bursting open, make sure the joins are well sealed with egg.

COOK'S TIP
Serve the dumplings straight from the oven. If they are allowed to cool, the apple shrinks back and looks rather sad when you cut through the pastry.

● 490 calories per portion

CHEAP AND CHEERFUL SUPPER

Here is a menu that conjures up a colorful and tasty meal for six without breaking the bank! The appetizer uses inexpensive seasonal vegetables served with an unusual hot dip, while the main course, an economical version of a traditional paella, is filling and substantial. A frothy citrus dessert is the perfect foil for the richer taste of the main course.

Cook's Notes

Smoky dip with vegetables

TIME
20 minutes to prepare the vegetables and 10-15 minutes to cook the dip.

ECONOMY
The tomato juice may be used in the Mock paella, if wished - add at stage 1 with the tomatoes.

COOK'S TIP
To ensure that the sauce is really smooth, put it back into the blender for a few seconds at this stage.

VARIATION
For a slightly more spicy dip, add a few drops of hot-pepper sauce.

● 135 calories per portion

Mock paella

TIME
15 minutes preparation, 35-40 minutes cooking.

SERVING IDEAS
The dish is a meal in itself, but serve with a green salad, if liked.

VARIATIONS
The ingredients can be varied according to taste and what stores you have to hand. For instance, try using left-over chicken or pork instead of the luncheon meat. Add a jar of drained mussels if your budget can stretch to it. A small can of whole kernel corn makes an interesting addition, too.

● 705 calories per portion

Smoky dip with vegetables

SERVES 6
¼ lb small mushrooms
1 large green pepper, seeded and cut into thin strips
4 carrots, cut into thin strips
1 cauliflower, broken into flowerets
1 bunch scallions

DIP
1 can (about 8 oz) tomatoes
⅔ cup milk
2 tablespoons butter or margarine
2 tablespoons all-purpose flour
1 teaspoon Dijon-style mustard
½-1 teaspoon chili powder
1 cup grated smoked cheese
black pepper

1 Make the dip: Drain the tomatoes (see Economy) and blend with the milk in a blender until smooth.
2 Melt the butter in a pan, sprinkle in the flour. Then add the mustard and chili powder to taste, and stir over low heat 1-2 minutes. Remove from the heat and gradually stir in the tomato and milk mixture. Return to the heat and simmer, stirring, until thick.
3 Add the grated cheese and stir over low heat until the cheese has melted (see Cook's tip).
4 Season to taste with pepper, transfer to a small serving bowl and place in the center of a large plate. Arrange the vegetables around the dip and serve while dip is warm.

Mock paella

SERVES 6

3 kabanos sausages, chopped into
  ½-inch lengths
1 can (about 11 oz) luncheon meat,
  cut into ½-inch dice
2 tablespoons vegetable oil
1 large onion, chopped
1 large red pepper, seeded and
  chopped
2 cloves garlic, crushed
  (optional)
6 oz smoked fatty bacon slices,
  chopped
3 tomatoes, peeled and chopped
1 teaspoon ground turmeric
1⅔ cups long-grain rice, rinsed
1½ cups frozen peas
2½-3 cups chicken broth
2 bay leaves
salt and freshly ground black
  pepper
1 can (about 7 oz) shrimp, drained
lemon wedges, to garnish

1 Heat the oil in a large skillet, add the onion, red pepper and garlic, if using, and cook gently 5 minutes until the onion is soft and lightly colored. Add the bacon and continue to cook for 3 minutes, then add the tomatoes and cook a further 5 minutes.

2 Add the chopped kabanos and luncheon meat and continue to cook, stirring, a further 2 minutes.

3 Stir in the turmeric, rice and frozen peas. Add about 2½ cups of the chicken broth, stir well and add the bay leaves. Season with salt and pepper to taste and simmer gently 20-25 minutes, stirring occasionally until the rice is tender and the liquid has been absorbed. Stir in the remaining broth, a little at a time, during cooking if the paella begins to look dry and the rice is not quite cooked.

4 Add the shrimp and stir until they are heated through. Discard the bay leaves, transfer the paella to a warmed serving dish and serve at once, garnished with lemon wedges.

Citrus snow

SERVES 6
1 small orange
1 lemon
1 lime
1¼ cups cold water
1 envelope unflavored gelatin
½ cup sugar
3 egg whites (see Economy)
candied orange and lemon slices, to decorate

1 Pour the cold water into a small saucepan and sprinkle in the gelatin. Leave to soak about 5 minutes.
2 Meanwhile, using a vegetable parer, thinly pare the rind from the orange, lemon and lime. Add to the spongy gelatin with the sugar.
3 Over low heat stir the mixture with a metal spoon until the sugar and gelatin have both dissolved. [!] Remove from the heat and leave to stand about 10 minutes.
4 Meanwhile, squeeze the juice from the orange, lemon and lime.
5 Put the gelatin mixture through a nylon strainer into a large bowl and add the squeezed fruit juices. Stir well, then refrigerate about 45 minutes, stirring occasionally, [!] until the mixture begins to thicken and turn syrupy.
6 Add the egg whites and beat until very thick (see Cook's tip). Turn into individual glasses and refrigerate for 3 hours.
7 Decorate the tops with candied orange and lemon slices just before serving up.

COUNTDOWN
In the morning
● Prepare the vegetables for the Smoky dip and refrigerate: Put the green pepper, cauliflower and scallions in a plastic bag, the carrots in a bowl of iced water and mushrooms in a covered bowl.
4 hours before
● Make Citrus snow; refrigerate.
1 hour before
● Make the Mock paella up to the end of stage 2.

15 minutes before
● Make the Smoky dip.
● Add the turmeric, rice, peas, broth and seasoning to the paella and simmer.
Just before the meal
● Transfer the dip to a serving dish and surround with the vegetables.
Just before the main course
● Stir the shrimp into the paella, garnish and serve.
Just before the dessert
● Decorate the Citrus snow.

Cook's Notes

TIME
25 minutes preparation, plus thickening and chilling time.

COOK'S TIP
Beating with an electric beater will take about 10 minutes. Do not be tempted to skimp on this operation; the mixture should be really fluffy and thick.

ECONOMY
If you do not want to use the left-over egg yolks straightaway, you can freeze them. Decide whether you want them for a sweet or savory dish and beat ¼ teaspoon sugar or salt into them. Pour into a small rigid container and freeze up to 6 months with salt and 8 months with sugar. Use as soon as thawed.

VARIATION
Use 3 lemons instead of the mixed fruits.

WATCHPOINTS
Do not allow the mixture to boil.
The mixture must be stirred occasionally to prevent it from setting at the base.

● 90 calories per portion

FREEZER DINNER

Make the most of your freezer with this delicious three-course meal! Scallops in tomato sauce, Orange chicken casserole and Frozen raspberry favorite, can be cooked in advance and stored in the freezer until required, leaving you free on the day to enjoy your own dinner party.

Scallops in tomato sauce

SERVES 6
12 cleaned scallops, fresh or frozen (see Cook's tips)
½ cup white wine or apple juice
½ cup water
1 bay leaf
10 peppercorns

SAUCE
1 small onion, finely chopped
1 small clove garlic, finely chopped (optional)
1 tablespoon olive oil or vegetable oil
1 lb tomatoes, peeled and chopped
pinch of sugar
2 teaspoons chopped fresh basil (optional)
1 teaspoon dried oregano
pinch of dried thyme
salt and freshly ground black pepper

TO GARNISH
¼ cup butter or margarine
1 lb potatoes, cooked and mashed
2-3 tablespoons warm milk

TO SERVE
2 tablespoons butter
2-3 tablespoons fine bread crumbs
1-2 tablespoons chopped fresh parsley

1 Bring the wine and water to a boil in a shallow pan with the bay leaf and peppercorns. Put in the scallops, cover the pan, and remove from the heat immediately, leaving the scallops in the liquid. [!]
2 Preheat the oven to 400°.
3 To make the sauce: Heat the oil in a pan, add onion and garlic, if using, and cook gently until soft and lightly colored. Add the tomatoes, sugar, herbs and salt and pepper to taste, then strain in the liquid from the scallops. Bring to a boil, then lower the heat and simmer about 15 minutes until sauce is thick and almost all liquid has evaporated.

4 Slice the scallops, stir them into the sauce, then taste and adjust seasoning. Spoon into individual ovenproof dishes or scallop shells.
5 To prepare the garnish: Beat the butter into the mashed potato and add enough warm milk to give a smooth creamy mixture, stiff enough to pipe. Spoon into a pastry bag fitted with a plain or star tip, then pipe a decorative border around each dish.
6 Allow the scallops to cool completely. Open-freeze until solid, then wrap and seal in plastic wrap and label and return to the freezer.
7 To serve: Unwrap and reheat from frozen in a 375° oven about 15 minutes. Remove from the oven, dot with the butter and sprinkle with the bread crumbs. Return to the oven a further 15 minutes or until the topping is golden brown. Serve at once, sprinkled with parsley.

COUNTDOWN
3 months before
● Make the chicken casserole and freeze. Make the ice cream mixture and the raspberry sauce and freeze.

1 month before
● Prepare the scallops and freeze.

The day before
● Take the chicken casserole out of the freezer and allow to thaw overnight at room temperature.

4 hours before
● Take the raspberry sauce out of the freezer.

30 minutes before
● Take the scallops out of the freezer and thaw in the oven.

Immediately before serving
● Take the ice cream mixture out of the freezer. Decorate and pour sauce into a pitcher.

Cook's Notes

TIME
Total preparation time before freezing is about 40 minutes. (Can be stored in the freezer for up to 1 month.) The scallops then take about 30 minutes to thaw and finish before serving.

COOK'S TIPS
If using fresh scallops, reserve 6 of the deepest shells for serving. Frozen scallops are available off the shell in large supermarkets, freezer centers and high-class fishmongers. Shells can be bought separately at fishmongers and specially kitchen stores. They can be kept and used again.

If using frozen scallops, there is no need to thaw them. Add them to the hot wine liquid while still frozen, but bring the liquid back to a boil before removing from heat.

WATCHPOINT
Like all shellfish, scallops need very little cooking or they will become tough. The standing time in the hot liquid plus the browning in the oven is sufficient to cook them through.

● 300 calories per portion

Orange chicken casserole

SERVES 6

6 chicken pieces
2 tablespoons all-purpose flour
salt and freshly ground black
  pepper
¼ cup butter or margarine
1 tablespoon vegetable oil
1¼ cups dry white wine
⅔ cup orange juice
½ teaspoon ground coriander
½ teaspoon dried tarragon or
  chervil

TO SERVE

⅔ cup heavy cream
2 large oranges, peeled and
  sliced
⅓ cup pitted black olives,
  halved

1 Put the flour in a plastic bag and season with salt and pepper. Wipe the chicken pieces dry with paper towels, place in the bag and shake until they are well coated.
2 Melt the butter with the oil in a large flameproof casserole and cook the chicken until golden.
3 Pour the wine and orange juice into the casserole and add the coriander, tarragon and salt and pepper to taste. Cover and simmer over a low heat about 45 minutes, or until the chicken is cooked.
4 Transfer chicken and sauce to a rigid container, leaving headspace. Cool quickly, seal, label and freeze.
5 To serve: Thaw in container overnight in the refrigerator, or 4-5 hours at room temperature. Turn into a flameproof casserole and reheat gently until bubbling, stirring occasionally, then cover and cook 10 minutes. Remove the chicken from the sauce with a slotted spoon, place in a warmed serving dish and keep hot. Boil the sauce until reduced, stir in the cream and adjust seasoning.
6 Pour the sauce over the chicken. Cut the orange slices in half, then arrange a few on the chicken and remainder around the dish. Scatter over olives and serve at once.

Cook's Notes

TIME
Allow about 75 minutes for preparation and cooking before freezing. (Can be stored in the freezer up to 3 months.) The chicken and sauce will take 4-5 hours or overnight to thaw then about 30 minutes to finish before serving.

● 490 calories per portion

Frozen raspberry favorite

SERVES 6

1¼ cups heavy cream
3 tablespoons kirsch or medium
 sweet sherry
8 ready-made meringue shells
 (see Buying guide), roughly
 broken
½ cup confectioners' sugar,
 sifted
1 lb fresh or frozen raspberries,
 thawed (see Variation)
vegetable oil, for greasing

TO SERVE

½ cup fresh or frozen raspberries,
 thawed

1 Brush the inside of an 8½ × 4½
× 2½ inches loaf pan with oil and
place in the bottom of the refrigerator to chill for 1 hour.
2 Beat the cream until it forms soft

peaks, then add the kirsch and beat
again until thickened.
3 Fold in the meringue pieces with
a metal spoon and 1 tablespoon of
the confectioners' sugar.
4 Turn the mixture into the chilled
pan, cover with foil, seal, label and
freeze.
5 Prepare the raspberry sauce:
Press the raspberries through a
sieve into a bowl, or work in a
blender. Stir in the sugar and mix
well. Pour into a rigid container,
seal, label and freeze.
6 To serve: Thaw the raspberry
sauce about 2-4 hours at room
temperature. Just before serving,
remove the ice cream from the
freezer and remove wrappings. Dip
the base of the pan into hot water 1-
2 seconds, then invert a serving
platter on top. Quickly invert the
pan onto the platter, giving a sharp
shake halfway round. Pour a little of
the sauce over the mold, decorate
with raspberries and serve at once.
Pour the remaining sauce into a
pitcher and hand separately.

Cook's Notes

TIME
Total preparation time,
including chilling the
pan, is 1½ hours. (Can be stored
in the freezer up to 3 months.)
After freezing, allow 2-4 hours to
thaw the raspberry sauce at room
temperature before serving.

BUYING GUIDE
Boxes of meringue
shells or nests are
readily available in most good
supermarkets and delicatessens.

VARIATION
Any summer fruit can
be used for this ice
cream instead of raspberries,
such as strawberries, red
currants or blackberries.

● 380 calories per portion

MEAL IN UNDER AN HOUR

Friends are coming round for dinner at short notice! Don't panic, just follow this super-quick, super-delicious menu: the ingredients are uncomplicated and the meal can be on the table in under an hour. Open with a light egg appetizer, follow with steaks in a luscious vermouth sauce, and end with Peach flambé – your guests will think you've spent hours in the kitchen!

Egg mayonnaise appetizer

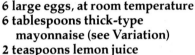

SERVES 4
6 large eggs, at room temperature
6 tablespoons thick-type
   mayonnaise (see Variation)
2 teaspoons lemon juice
¼ teaspoon dry mustard
salt and freshly ground black pepper

GARNISH
4 lettuce leaves
paprika

1 Put the eggs in a saucepan and cover with water. Bring to a boil then lower the heat and simmer gently 8-10 minutes. Drain off water and hold the pan under cold running water to cool the eggs quickly. As soon as the eggs are cool enough to handle, tap each one once against a hard surface to crack the shell, then cool (see Cook's tip).

2 Put the mayonnaise in a bowl and stir in the lemon juice, mustard and salt and pepper to taste.

3 Remove the shells from the cold eggs, then slice the eggs. Reserve 8 slices and chop the rest. Mix the chopped egg into the mayonnaise.

4 Arrange the lettuce leaves on individual serving plates and spoon the egg mixture onto them. Garnish each portion with 2 egg slices and sprinkle with paprika.

Steak with vermouth sauce

SERVES 4
4 beef steaks (see Buying guide)
freshly ground black pepper
2 tablespoons butter or margarine
1 tablespoon vegetable oil
sprigs of watercress, to garnish

SAUCE
2 tablespoons butter
⅔ cup red vermouth
½ teaspoon French grainy mustard
salt

1 Sprinkle the steaks with pepper on both sides.
2 Heat the butter and oil in a large skillet add the steaks and cook over brisk heat until browned on both sides, turning once. Remove

the steaks from the pan with a slotted spoon, arrange on a warmed serving platter and keep hot.
3 Make the sauce: Melt the butter in the pan over moderate heat. When it begins to froth, stir in the vermouth, mustard and salt and pepper to taste. Boil quickly until the liquid has become slightly syrupy.
4 Pour the sauce immediately over the steaks, garnish with watercress and serve at once.

Cook's Notes

Egg mayonnaise appetizer

TIME
35 minutes to cook and cool the eggs, then 10 minutes preparation.

COOK'S TIP
Cracking the shell will prevent a dark rim forming around the yolk.

VARIATION
Homemade mayonnaise made with olive oil will give a richer flavor to the dish.

SERVING IDEAS
The egg mayonnaise can also be served on points of buttered brown bread. Garnish with chopped walnuts and watercress. Or, serve it in stemmed glasses on shredded lettuce, layered with well-drained chopped tomato and cucumber.

● 280 calories per portion

Steak with vermouth sauce

TIME
10 minutes preparation and cooking time in total.

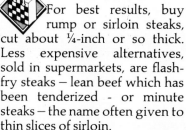

BUYING GUIDE
For best results, buy rump or sirloin steaks, cut about ¼-inch or so thick. Less expensive alternatives, sold in supermarkets, are flash-fry steaks — lean beef which has been tenderized - or minute steaks — the name often given to thin slices of sirloin.

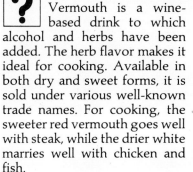

SERVING IDEAS
Serve the steaks with small potatoes baked in their jackets, a frozen vegetable and baked tomatoes. Alternatively, serve with garlic bread and a fresh green salad, tossed in a dressing.

DID YOU KNOW
Vermouth is a wine-based drink to which alcohol and herbs have been added. The herb flavor makes it ideal for cooking. Available in both dry and sweet forms, it is sold under various well-known trade names. For cooking, the sweeter red vermouth goes well with steak, while the drier white marries well with chicken and fish.

● 455 calories per portion

COUNTDOWN
50 minutes before
● Put the potatoes in the oven (see Serving ideas) or prepare the garlic bread and green salad.
● Put the eggs onto boil for the Egg mayonnaise appetizer, and prepare the mayonnaise mixture; cover and refrigerate.
35 minutes before
● Drain the eggs, crack the shells, then leave to cool.
● Start making the Peach flambé: Dissolve the sugar in the butter, stir in the wine, add the peaches and remove the pan from the heat. Set aside until needed.

15 minutes before
● Bake the tomatoes, if using, or put the garlic bread in the oven.
10 minutes before
● Complete the Egg mayonnaise appetizer and refrigerate until needed.
● Put the frozen vegetables on to cook, if using.
Just before the main course
● Cook the steak, make the sauce, pour over the steak, garnish and serve.
Just before the dessert
● Warm the brandy, reheat the peaches, flambé and serve sprinkled with walnuts.

Peach flambé

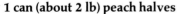

SERVES 4

1 can (about 2 lb) peach halves
4 tablespoons brandy
¼ cup sweet butter
¼ cup superfine sugar
⅓ cup medium-dry white
   wine
1 tablespoon finely chopped shelled
   walnuts

1 Drain the peaches well (see Cook's tip).
2 Pour the brandy into a cup and stand in a pan or bowl of hot water to warm through gently.
3 Melt the butter in a large, heavy-based pan. Add the sugar and cook over low heat, stirring occasionally, until the sugar has dissolved.
4 Stir in the wine, bring the mixture to a gentle simmer and add the peaches. Turn the peaches several times in the liquid to heat through and absorb the flavor. ⚠
5 Remove the pan from the heat, poor the warmed brandy over the peaches and set alight..
6 Allow the flames to die down, spoon into individual bowls and sprinkle with the walnuts. Serve.

Cook's Notes

 TIME
This special party dish takes just 15 minutes to prepare and serve.

⚠ **WATCHPOINT**
Turn the peaches gently with a fish slice and a spatula so that they do not break up.
   When lighting the brandy, stand well back and hold the match just above the side of the pan.

 SERVING IDEAS
Serve with whipped cream or ice cream and wafers or thin sweet cookies.

COOK'S TIP
The canned syrup is too sweet to be used in the flambé sauce. If stored, covered, in the refrigerator it will keep 2-3 days. Use it as the liquid for poaching fresh fruit.

● 400 calories per portion

BUDGET DINNER

A budget dinner need not mean a dull dinner. With a little forethought and imagination, some of the most delicious dishes can be made from the most economical of ingredients – and without spending hours in the kitchen. This menu of home-made soup, kabobs with rice and a barbecue sauce, and a meringue dessert is both economical and impressive.

Nearly all home-made soups are less expensive than bought ones, and also have infinitely better flavor. So impress your guests by making a soup such as creamy watercress, which is not only economical, but unobtainable from a package or can.

For the main course of the meal, show just what can be done with ground beef by making it into mouthwatering kabobs topped with a spicy sauce. Cut main course costs even further by choosing the best of the vegetables in season to accompany the kabobs. Budget desserts are often uninspiring, but not this Meringue dessert, an English dish which is a perfect all-year standby, most useful in the dark days of winter when there are few interesting and inexpensive fresh fruits in season.

When entertaining, it is always important, and polite, to know your guests' likes and dislikes. This is particularly so with budget food – many bargain buys are cheap simply because they are not popular! If you know what to buy, and how to prepare it – then your family and friends will be in for a pleasant surprise and a tasty treat.

Creamy watercress soup

SERVES 4
2 bunches watercress
1 medium onion, quartered
2½ cups well-flavored chicken broth (preferably homemade, see Economy)
1 teaspoon lemon juice
salt and freshly ground black pepper
2 tablespoons cornstarch
1¼ cups milk
pinch of freshly ground nutmeg

Cook's Notes

 TIME
This soup takes 45 minutes to make.

 VARIATION
Substitute 1 package (about 9 oz) frozen leaf or chopped spinach for watercress.

 ECONOMY
To be even more economical, and improve the flavor, make your own broth from left-over chicken carcass.

 COOK'S TIP
A quick way to blend cornstarch and milk without first making a paste is to whizz it for a few seconds in the blender, after puréeing the soup.

● 95 calories per portion

1 Put watercress into a saucepan, reserving a few sprigs for the garnish. Add the onion, chicken broth, lemon juice and salt and pepper to taste.
2 Bring to a boil, then lower the heat, cover the pan and simmer 30 minutes. Remove from the heat and leave to cool slightly.
3 Work the soup to a smooth purée in a blender or rub through a sieve.
4 Return the soup to the rinsed-out pan. Mix cornstarch to a paste with a little of the milk, then stir in the remaining milk. Stir this mixture slowly into the soup, then bring to a boil, stirring all the time. Simmer for 2 minutes.
5 Add the nutmeg, taste and adjust seasoning, then pour into warmed individual soup bowls. Serve piping hot, garnished with watercress sprigs.

Beefball and apricot kabobs

SERVES 4
1 lb lean ground beef
1 small onion, grated
½ cup fresh white bread crumbs
½ teaspoon ground ginger
¼ teaspoon dried thyme
½ teaspoon salt
¼ teaspoon freshly ground black pepper
1 egg, lightly beaten
6 slices fatty bacon, cut in half
6 large dried apricots, halved

BARBECUE SAUCE
3 tablespoons wine vinegar
2 tablespoons light brown sugar
2 tablespoons tomato catsup
2 tablespoons fruit chutney
2 teaspoons cornstarch
2 teaspoons soy sauce
1¼ cups water
salt and freshly ground black pepper

1 Preheat broiler to high.
2 Mix together the beef, onion, bread crumbs, ginger, thyme and salt and pepper. Add the egg, then mix with your hands until combined (see Cook's tip). Shape into 16 balls.
3 Wrap each bacon slice around each apricot half.
4 Thread the meatballs and apricots in bacon alternately onto 4 skewers, allowing 4 meatballs and 3 apricots in bacon for each. ✳
5 Broil the kabobs 7-10 minutes, turning them over frequently until browned and cooked through. !
6 Meanwhile, make the sauce: Put all the ingredients into a saucepan and bring to boil, stirring constantly. Boil 2 minutes.
7 Serve at once on a bed of rice, with the sauce poured over.

Cook's Notes

TIME
The kabobs take 35 minutes.

COOK'S TIP
Mixing the meat with your hands is quick and makes it easier to shape.

BUYING GUIDE
Make sure you buy really lean ground beef for this dish. Fatty ground beef will make the meatballs shrink and lose their shape when cooked, so it is a false economy.

WATCHPOINT
If the kabobs look as if they are going to burn, reduce the heat and continue to broil until they are cooked through. Remember to keep turning them frequently.

FREEZING
The uncooked kabobs can be frozen on their skewers for up to 1 month, wrapped individually in foil or plastic wrap. To use, unwrap and broil from frozen for about 15 minutes. Uncooked meatballs can be frozen individually, then packed together in a plastic bag or rigid container. They can then be used for quick family snacks and suppers since you can take out only as many as you need.

● 525 calories per portion

Meringue dessert

SERVES 4
6 oz pie crust sticks

FILLING
1¼ cups milk
grated rind of 1 lemon
1 cup fresh white bread crumbs
2 medium eggs, separated
¼ cup butter or margarine
½ cup superfine sugar
1 teaspoon vanilla
3 tablespoons raspberry jelly

Cook's Notes

TIME
Preparation time about 30 minutes, including time for making fresh pastry. Allow an extra 30 minutes for the pastry to chill before using. Baking time is 1 hour.

WATCHPOINTS
Take care when putting the pie in the oven with the uncooked filling; it is fairly runny and can easily spill over onto the cookie sheet.

Beat the egg whites for the meringue topping immediately before they are put on the pudding. If beaten in advance they will deflate, and become watery.

Make sure the meringue touches the pastry all round or it will shrink back during cooking and look unsightly.

COOK'S TIP
The quantities given here will produce at least 4 ample portions. Any left-over pudding is delicious cold.

● 535 calories per portion

1 Preheat the oven to 350°.
2 Roll out the dough on a floured board and use to line an 8 inch flan ring standing on a cookie sheet. Set aside to rest while you prepare the filling.
3 Bring the milk to a boil in a saucepan, remove from the heat, then add the lemon rind, bread crumbs, yolks, butter, ¼ cup sugar and the vanilla. Stir well with a wooden spoon until the bread crumbs have absorbed most of the milk. Leave to cool.
4 Spread jelly over the base of the uncooked pie shell, then pour all of the bread crumb mixture on top. !
5 Bake in the oven 45 minutes until the filling is set, then carefully remove the flan ring.
6 Beat the egg whites until they stand in soft peaks. Fold in the remaining sugar with a metal spoon, then pile the meringue on top of the cooked pudding. !
7 Return to the oven and bake a further 15 minutes, or until the meringue is browned. Transfer to a serving plate and serve either warm or cold.

COCKTAIL PARTY

Inviting a few friends round for drinks? Why not be adventurous — and serve cocktails? Choose one or two from the chart on page 74, offer them with our two sophisticated nibbles, and your evening is sure to be a wild success!

Mixing cocktails

The ingredients for cocktails are either stirred or shaken together. Traditionally, a cocktail shaker is used for shaking the ingredients, and many of these have built-in strainers, but rather than going to the expense of buying one especially for this occasion, you can easily improvise with a tight-lidded jar and a small strainer.

To shake a cocktail, put enough crushed ice into the shaker to cover the base to a depth of about 1 inch. Then add the ingredients, shake and strain into the glass.

Crushed ice is often a vital ingredient of the drink — to prepare the ice, either crush ice cubes in a strong blender or food processor, or put ice in a strong plastic bag and crush with a wooden mallet or rolling pin.

A proper cocktail measure is very helpful, but a standard measuring cup and spoon can be used if the ingredients are kept in the proportions given in the recipes. As a guide remember that a measure normally equals 2 tablespoons.

The proportions given on page 74 are for one serving only.

Hot cheese and crab dip

SERVES 12
1½ cups grated sharp Cheddar cheese
¼ cup butter or margarine
½ cup all-purpose flour
2 cups milk
1 tablespoon lemon juice
1 teaspoon Worcestershire sauce
1 teaspoon Dijon-style mustard
salt and freshly ground black pepper
2-3 tablespoons finely chopped canned pimiento
2-3 tablespoons finely chopped green pepper
6 black olives, pitted and finely chopped
4 tablespoons dry white wine
1 can (about 6 oz) crabmeat, drained and all cartilage removed

TO SERVE
small Melba toast squares
small cubes of French bread
small savory crackers

1 Melt the butter in a saucepan, sprinkle in the flour and stir over low heat 1-2 minutes until straw-colored. Remove from the heat and gradually stir in the milk. Return to the heat and simmer, stirring, until thick and smooth.
2 Remove from the heat and stir in the cheese until melted and smooth. Add the lemon juice, Worcestershire sauce, mustard and salt and pepper to taste and mix well.
3 Stir in the pimiento, green pepper, olives, wine and crabmeat, then heat through gently, stirring.
4 Pour into a warmed serving dish. Serve at once with small Melba toast squares, cubes of French bread and savory crackers (see Cook's tip).

Cook's Notes

TIME
10 minutes preparation; 10 minutes cooking.

COOK'S TIP
This dip is best if served piping hot. If possible, stand it on a warmed serving tray or hostess trolley.

● 160 calories per portion

Chili meat balls

MAKES 36-40
1 lb lean ground beef
2 tablespoons tomato catsup
2 tablespoons mild chili sauce
1 tablespoon Worcestershire sauce
1 cup cornflakes, finely crushed
½ cup canned evaporated milk
salt and freshly ground black pepper
vegetable oil, for greasing

DIPPING SAUCE
5 tablespoons tomato catsup
3 tablespoons mild chili sauce
1 tablespoon lemon juice
¾ teaspoon creamed horseradish
¾ teaspoon Worcestershire sauce
few drops of hot-pepper sauce

1 Preheat the oven to 400°. Grease 2 cookie sheets with oil.
2 Place the beef in a large bowl together with the tomato catsup, chili sauce, Worcestershire sauce, cornflakes and evaporated milk. Season with salt and pepper to taste, then mix well together with your fingers.
3 Shape the beef mixture into about 40 bite-sized meat balls (see Cook's tip) and arrange on the greased cookie sheets. Cook in the oven 15-20 minutes or until browned.
4 Meanwhile, make the sauce: Put the tomato catsup in a small serving bowl and stir in the rest of the sauce ingredients. Place the bowl of sauce in the center of a large platter.
5 Serve the meat balls on a warmed serving dish accompanied by the dipping sauce (see Serving ideas).

Cook's Notes

TIME
The meat balls take about 10 minutes preparation, then 15-20 minutes cooking.

COOK'S TIP
The meat balls should be about the same size as walnuts, so that they are easy to eat in one mouthful.

SERVING IDEAS
Provide wooden or colored plastic toothpicks so that the meat balls can be dipped into the sauce and eaten without difficulty.

● 130 calories per portion

COCKTAILS

COCKTAIL	INGREDIENTS	METHOD	TO SERVE
Gin-based:			
Boxcar	3 tablespoons gin 3 tablespoons Cointreau 1 teaspoon lime juice 1 egg white 1-2 dashes grenadine	Put all ingredients in shaker with crushed ice and shake well	First frost rim of champagne glass: dip glass into beaten egg white and then superfine sugar. Strain cocktail into glass
Gimlet	¼ cup gin 2 teaspoons sweetened lime juice	Put ingredients in shaker with crushed ice and shake well	Strain into old-fashioned type glass and add ice cubes
Martini	¼ cup gin 1-2 teaspoons dry vermouth	Stir ingredients together	Serve in chilled cocktail glass garnished with an olive or twist of lemon rind
Bourbon or whiskey-based:			
Horse's Neck	5 tablespoons whiskey few drops of lemon juice ginger ale	Stir whiskey and lemon juice together, then add ice cubes and fill glass with ginger ale	Serve in a highball glass garnished with a long spiral of lemon rind
Manhattan	5 tablespoons whiskey 2 tablespoons sweet vermouth	Stir ingredients together	Serve in cocktail glass garnished with maraschino cherry
Vodka-based:			
Black Russian	3 tablespoons vodka 1½ tablespoons coffee liqueur	Put ingredients in shaker with crushed ice and shake well	Strain into an old-fashioned type glass and add crushed ice.
Bloody Mary	3 tablespoons vodka 6 tablespoons tomato juice 1 tablespoon lemon juice dash of Worcestershire sauce few drops of hot-pepper sauce salt and black pepper	Put all ingredients in shaker with crushed ice and shake well. Strain and season to taste with salt and pepper	Serve in tall glass garnished with stick of cucumber and mint sprigs or lemon wedge
Harvey Wallbanger	2 tablespoons vodka orange juice 2 teaspoons galliano	Put vodka in glass, add ice cubes and fill with orange juice. Stir, then float galliano on top	Serve in tall glass
Rum-based:			
Between the sheets	2 tablespoons rum 2 tablespoons brandy 2 tablespoons Cointreau 1 teaspoon lemon juice	Put all ingredients in shaker with crushed ice and shake well	Strain into an old-fashioned type glass and add crushed ice
Daiquiri	¼ cup white rum 2 tablespoons lime juice 1 teaspoon sugar syrup	Put all ingredients in shaker with crushed ice and shake well	Strain into cocktail glass and add crushed ice
Tequila-based:			
Marguerita	¼ cup tequila 2 teaspoons Cointreau 1 tablespoon lime juice	Place all ingredients in shaker with crushed ice and shake well	Frost rim of cocktail glass: dip glass into lime juice and then salt. Strain cocktail into glass
Tequila Sunrise	¼ cup tequila ½ cup orange juice 2 teaspoons grenadine	Put tequila in glass, add ice cubes and fill glass with orange juice. Stir. Slowly pour in grenadine so it settles on bottom of glass	Serve in tall glass garnished with lemon slice. Stir cocktail before drinking

FESTIVE MEAL

This menu has been created to serve on that special festive occasion when traditional charm and flavor are appropriate. The meal begins with a melon and shrimp cocktail that is suitably light and refreshing before the main course of stuffed turkey which is half boned to make carving easier. The dessert is impressively flambéed with the added surprise of a fruity, creamy center. So, gather your friends and celebrate with our festive meal.

Melon and shrimp cocktail

SERVES 8

1 small honeydew melon, seeded and pared
2 tablespoons red wine vinegar
4 tablespoons vegetable oil
1 teaspoon Dijon-style mustard
1 tablespoon chopped fresh parsley
salt and freshly ground black pepper
1 large red dessert apple
3 celery stalks, thinly sliced
1½ cups peeled shrimp
8 unpeeled shrimp, to garnish

1 Put the vinegar, oil, mustard and parsley into a bowl. Season with salt and pepper. Beat well.
2 Cut the melon into small neat cubes. Quarter and core the apple but do not pare it, then cut the flesh into neat cubes.
3 Put the melon, celery, apple and shrimp into the dressing and mix lightly together. Spoon the melon and shrimp mixture into 6 serving glasses. Garnish and serve at once.

Festive turkey

SERVES 8

9 lb turkey, boned (see Buying guide and Preparation)
⅓ cup butter, softened
2 tablespoons all-purpose flour
2½ cups turkey broth, made from the giblets and bones
sliced red and green pepper, to garnish

STUFFING

1 tablespoon corn oil
1 large onion, finely chopped
1 small red pepper, seeded and chopped
1 small green pepper, seeded and chopped
1 cup chopped lean ham
3 cups fresh white bread crumbs
2 teaspoons dried mixed herbs
3 tablespoons chopped fresh parsley
1 lb pork sausagemeat
1 egg
salt and freshly ground black pepper

1 Make the stuffing: Heat the oil in a large skillet, add the onion and peppers and cook gently 5 minutes until the onion is soft and lightly colored. Cool completely.
2 Put the ham, bread crumbs, herbs, sausagemeat and egg into a large bowl. Add the onion and peppers and season well with salt and pepper. Mix thoroughly together.
3 Preheat the oven to 375°.
4 Lay the boned turkey out flat on a board, skin-side down, and tuck in the small pieces of wing. Then trim off the excess skin at the neck and season the turkey well with salt and pepper. Stuff the body cavity and upper part of the legs where the bone has gone (to stop legs collapsing during roasting). Bring the sides of the turkey neatly up and over the stuffing to enclose it completely.
5 Using a large trussing needle and fine string, neatly sew up the turkey along the backbone where it was cut, to seal in the stuffing.
6 Turn the turkey over so that it is breast side up again. Press into a neat shape and tie the legs tightly together. Spread the skin with the softened butter and season with salt and pepper.
7 Wrap tightly in foil, put in roasting pan and roast 2½ hours.
8 Remove the foil from the turkey and continue to roast 60 minutes until the turkey is tender and the juices run clear when the thickest part of the thigh is pierced with a skewer.
9 Transfer the turkey to a warmed serving platter and allow to stand at least 30 minutes to firm up before carving.
10 Meanwhile, make the gravy: Drain off all the fat from the roasting pan, leaving behind the turkey juices. Sprinkle in the flour and cook over low heat until lightly colored. Stir in the broth and bring to a boil, scraping up all the sediment from the base of the pan. Reduce the heat slightly and simmer gently for 10-15 minutes. Strain into a warmed sauceboat.
11 Just before serving, remove the string from the turkey and garnish with red and green pepper slices. To serve, carve into slices, cutting right across the bird. Remove the legs in the normal way.

Cook's Notes

Melon and shrimp cocktail

TIME
This light appetizer takes 20 minutes to prepare.

● 120 calories per portion

Festive turkey

TIME
2 hours preparation, then 3½ hours roasting.

PREPARATION
To bone the turkey, first cut off the parson's nose.

1 Place the turkey breast-side down and cut through skin all along backbone. Carefully scrape flesh away from carcass, close to ribs, cutting thighs and wings free.

2 To remove top leg bone and top wing bone, scrape flesh from all round bones, then break ball and socket joints and pull out top bones. Repeat on other side. Ease knife between skin and breastbone and lift out the carcass. Do not cut through breast skin.

BUYING GUIDE
Boning is fairly difficult but becomes easier with practice. Use a fresh turkey, as the skin of a frozen bird is more likely to break. You can ask your butcher to bone it, but give him plenty of advance warning.

● 820 calories per portion

Flambéed ice cream dessert

SERVES 8

¼ cup candied cherries
⅓ cup dried apricots
⅓ cup pitted dates
2 tablespoons golden raisins
2 tablespoons seedless raisins
2 tablespoons candied peel
6 tablespoons brandy
2 cups heavy cream
⅔ cup sifted confectioners' sugar
1 teaspoon vanilla

CHOCOLATE COATING
6 squares (6 oz) semisweet chocolate
  broken into small pieces
2 tablespoons water
2 tablespoons butter

1 Cut the cherries, apricots and dates into small pieces, then put them in a bowl with the raisins and peel.
2 Add half the brandy to fruits and mix well. Cover and leave to stand at least 2 hours, stirring occasionally, until the fruits have softened and absorbed all the alcohol.
3 Pour the cream into a bowl, add confectioners' sugar and vanilla and beat until the cream forms soft peaks. Fold in the soaked fruits.
4 Spoon the cream mixture into a 1 quart pudding bowl and smooth the top. Cover with plastic wrap and freeze 4-5 hours until frozen solid.
5 Remove from the freezer, then dip a spatula in hot water and run around the edge of the dessert. Place a round of foil on top of the pudding, turn out onto a small wire rack and return to the freezer while you are preparing the chocolate coating.
6 Put the chocolate, water and butter in a heatproof bowl. Set the bowl over a pan half full of simmering water and leave, stirring occasionally, until the chocolate is melted.
7 Remove the dessert from the freezer and place the rack over a plate. Pour the chocolate coating over the frozen pudding, smoothing it round the sides with a spatula to coat it completely — the chocolate does not have to be completely smooth. Return to the freezer until

chocolate hardens. ✳
8 Pour remaining brandy into a pan and heat through gently.
9 To serve: Remove the dessert from the freezer, peel off the foil round the base and place the pudding on a serving plate. Set light

to the warmed brandy and pour, flaming, over the dessert. Allow to flame until the chocolate starts to bubble round the base, then blow out the flames and serve.

Cook's Notes

TIME
30 minutes to prepare, plus 2 hours soaking the fruit and 4½-5½ hours freezing.

FREEZING
Wrap in plastic wrap and foil then seal, label and freeze up to 3 months. To serve: unwrap and flame as described in recipe.

COOK'S TIP
This spectacular dessert gives the impression that a great deal of skill is needed to produce it — but it is, in fact, very simple, although time-consuming, to make.

● 515 calories per portion

COUNTDOWN
2 days before
● Make and freeze the Flambéed iced cream dessert.
The day before
● Bone the turkey and make the turkey broth.
In the morning
● Thaw the shrimp for the Melon and shrimp cocktail.
● Make the stuffing for the Festive turkey, stuff the turkey and sew up.
3½ hours before
● Roast the turkey.
20 minutes before
● Prepare the Melon and shrimp cocktail.
Just before the meal
● Transfer the turkey to a platter.
Just before the main course
● Make the gravy and carve turkey.
Just before the dessert
● Remove the pudding from the freezer, heat the brandy, ignite and pour over the pudding.

BARBECUE PARTY

A barbecue party is the perfect way to relax with friends on a warm summer's evening. Cooking in the open is a lot of fun, and so easy to organize – less washing up for you, and guests can join in with the cooking! Try our exotic selection of three spicy dishes using marinated pork, chicken and lamb from which guests can pick and choose. Accompany them with an unusual Coconut rice salad and finish with a refreshing Orange and lemon water-ice.

BARBECUE KNOW-HOW

Equipment: There are many portable barbecues which can be bought or hired, but you can improvise by building your own with bricks or using a container such as a garden refuse burner. All you really need is a hole for the draught to keep the fire burning and a grid (oven shelves are ideal).

Fuel: Always use charcoal for burning. This can be bought in bags from hardware stores, garden centers and some large supermarkets. Briquettes are more expensive than ordinary charcoal pieces, but they usually burn for longer and are, therefore, more economical in the long run – they are also less messy to use. You will also need a stock of firelighters.

Tools: Long-handled barbecue tool sets, which usually comprise tongs, a spatula and a two-pronged fork, are a must for easy handling of food – and for safety; they are widely available and inexpensive.

Other general utensils: You will need a brush for brushing oil or marinade onto the food to keep it moist during barbecuing, and prevent it sticking to the grid; long metal skewers for kabobs; a slotted spoon for removing meat from marinades and pot holders for protecting your hands and paper towels for mopping up.

Lighting the barbecue: Light the charcoal 45-60 minutes before you intend to cook. The simplest way to light the coals is to mound them up in a pyramid in the center of the barbecue and insert some firelighters in between the coals. Barbecue lighting fluid can also be used – it is very efficient; so too are special barbecue pokers, but these are expensive and only worth buying if you intend to do a lot of barbecuing. When the flames have subsided and the coals look gray or

glow red in the dark, you can start cooking. Always oil the grid before starting to cook.

Cooking: a constant eye must be kept on the food to make sure that it does not burn. For a party to serve

12 people such as this one, it is unlikely that all the meats will fit on the grid at the same time so the food will have to be cooked in batches — the idea of our menu is that guests can pick and choose from the selection of meats and cook their own at their leisure.

Since appetites will be stimulated in the open air, it is a good idea to serve lots of accompaniments with the barbecued meat. The rice dish we suggest is a good filler and the Indian flavor combines well with the spiciness of the meat. A selection of different salads would make a refreshing addition. Potatoes wrapped in foil and baked over the grid are delicious served with dairy sour cream, or try barbecuing parcels of vegetables, such as drained canned whole kernel corn or sliced mushrooms, mixed with a little butter.

A clever tip for creating an extra herby flavor, is to sprinkle the hot coals with mixed dried herbs.

COUNTDOWN
2-3 days before
● Make the Orange and lemon water-ice.

The day before
● Prepare the coconut and cook the rice for the Coconut rice salad.
4 hours before
● Prepare the 3 marinades.
● Put the chicken, pork and lamb in their marinades.
1 hour before
● Light the barbecue.
● Mix the dressing for rice salad.
15 minutes before
● Begin cooking on the barbecue.
● Mix together all the ingredients for the Coconut rice salad.
Just before serving
● Take water-ice out of the freezer.

Curried pork

SERVES 12

3 pork tenderloins, total weight about 2½ lb, trimmed and halved lengthwise (see Buying guide)

MARINADE

8 tablespoons vegetable oil
2 tablespoons curry powder
2 tablespoons tomato paste
1 large onion, finely chopped
salt and freshly ground black pepper

1 First make the marinade: Put the oil into a large bowl with the curry powder, tomato paste, onion and salt and pepper to taste. Mix well.
2 Cut each tenderloin half into bite-sized pieces.
3 Put the meat into the marinade and stir well to make sure each piece is well coated. Cover and leave to marinate in a cool place at least 3 hours.
4 Thread the pork pieces onto 12 oiled skewers, reserving any marinade left in the bowl.
5 To cook: Place the skewers on the oiled grid and barbecue about 10 minutes until cooked through, turning several times and brushing occasionally with any reserved marinade during cooking.

Chicken in yogurt and ginger

SERVES 12

12 boneless skinned chicken breasts, each weighing about 5 oz
vegetable oil, for brushing

MARINADE

1¼ cups plain yogurt
2 tablespoons finely chopped fresh root ginger (see Buying guide), or 2 teaspoons ground ginger
½ teaspoon ground cardamom
½ teaspoon cayenne pepper
2 tablespoons finely chopped fresh coriander or parsley
1 teaspoon salt
2 cloves garlic, crushed (optional)

1 Put all the marinade ingredients, including the garlic, if using, into a large bowl and then stir them all well to mix.
2 Pat the chicken breasts dry with paper towels, then place in the marinade, making sure they are well coated. Cover and leave to marinate in a cool place at least 3 hours.
3 To cook: Remove the chicken breasts from the marinade with a slotted spoon, place on the oiled grid and barbecue about 10 minutes until cooked through, turning several times. Brush occasionally with oil during cooking.

Spiced lamb

SERVES 12

12 lean lamb chops, each weighing about ¼ lb
vegetable oil, for brushing

DRY MARINADE

1 tablespoon finely chopped fresh root ginger, or 1 teaspoon ground ginger
2 cloves garlic, crushed (optional)
1 teaspoon ground cardamom
½ teaspoon ground cinnamon
1 teaspoon ground cumin
¼ teaspoon cayenne pepper
2 teaspoons ground turmeric
salt and freshly ground black pepper

1 First make the dry marinade: Mix the ginger and garlic, if using, in a shallow dish with all the spices and plenty of salt and pepper.
2 Place the lamb chops in the dish and turn them in the spice mixture to make sure each chop is well coated. Cover the dish and leave to marinate in a cool place for at least 3 hours.
3 To cook: Place the chops on the oiled grid and barbecue 10-15 minutes until cooked through, turning several times with tongs and a fork. Brush occasionally with oil during cooking.

Cook's Notes

Curried pork
TIME
15 minutes to prepare, then at least 3 hours to marinate, 10 minutes cooking.

BUYING GUIDE
Pork tenderloin is an expensive cut, but there is so little fat on it that it is not so uneconomical as it may seem at first. Each tenderloin weighs about ¾ lb.

● 235 calories per portion

Chicken in yogurt and ginger
TIME
20 minutes to prepare, then at least 3 hours to marinate, 10 minutes cooking.

BUYING GUIDE
You can buy fresh root ginger and coriander at some farm markets and larger supermarkets. Peel fresh ginger with a vegetable parer before chopping.

● 190 calories per portion

Spiced lamb
TIME
10 minutes to prepare, then at least 3 hours to marinate and 10-15 minutes cooking.

● 175 calories per portion

Coconut rice salad

SERVES 12

1 lb long-grain rice
salt
3 chicken bouillon cubes, crumbled
2 teaspoons cumin seeds
1 small coconut, broken open and flesh removed (see Preparation), or 1 package (about ½ lb) shredded coconut
4 tablespoons corn or vegetable oil
2 tablespoons red wine vinegar
3 tablespoons finely chopped fresh parsley
¼ teaspoon dry mustard
freshly ground black pepper
3 bananas
1 cup salted peanuts

1 Fill a large saucepan with salted water and add crumbled bouillon cubes. Bring to a boil, then add the rice and cumin seeds. Stir once to mix the ingredients together, then cover and simmer gently 20-25 minutes until the rice is tender.

2 Pour the cooked rice into a strainer and rinse well under cold running water. Leave to cool and drain well.

3 Meanwhile, grate the coconut flesh finely.

4 Put the oil in a large serving bowl with vinegar, parsley, mustard and pepper to taste. Mix well.

5 Just before serving: Pare the bananas and slice them directly into the dressing. Mix lightly. Add the rice, grated coconut and peanuts ⚠ and fork lightly together.

Cook's Notes

TIME
About 40 minutes to prepare, including cooking the rice, plus about 1 hour to prepare the coconut most of which can be done while the rice is cooking.

WATCHPOINT
Add the peanuts just before serving or they will go soggy if left to stand in the dressing for some time.

PREPARATION
To prepare the coconut, first make holes in 2-3 'eyes' of the coconut with a screwdriver; drain off 'milk'.

Give the coconut a sharp blow with a mallet or small hammer. Tap all the way round until the shell breaks. Break up the coconut into manageable pieces and dig out flesh with a knife.

● 385 calories per portion

until it has frozen to a width of about 1 inch around the edge, then remove from the freezer and stir well with a large metal spoon until evenly blended. Return to the freezer and freeze a further 3 hours or until the water-ice is frozen to a firm mushy consistency, not completely hard. Stir with a metal spoon once every hour during this freezing process.

8 Fill the orange cases with the water-ice, mounding it up well on top. Replace the "lids", pressing them in at an angle. Return the oranges to the freezer for 1-2 hours or until the water-ice is frozen.

9 When ready to serve, remove the oranges from the freezer and place on small decorative plates or saucers. Serve at once.

Cook's Notes

 TIME
About 2 hours to make and 8-9 hours to freeze.

 WATCHPOINT
Be careful not to split the skins of the oranges when squeezing out the juice.

 BUYING GUIDE
Choose oranges with good umarked skins and try to find 12 more or less the same size.

 COOK'S TIP
If the orange cases do not stand level, take a very thin slice off the bases.

 PREPARATION
To remove all flesh from inside the oranges:

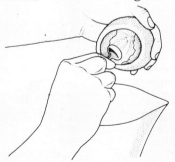

Use a teaspoon to scrape out all the flesh from the orange shells.

● 190 calories per portion

Orange and lemon water-ice

SERVES 12

 12 oranges (see Buying guide)
8-9 lemons
1 cup water
2 cups sugar

1 Set the refrigerator or freezer at its coldest setting.

2 Wash the oranges and 3 of the lemons. With a vegetable parer, pare the rind from the 3 lemons thinly, then put them into a saucepan with the water and sugar. Stir over a low heat until the sugar has dissolved, then bring to a boil. Boil for 2 minutes, without stirring, remove from the heat, cover and leave the syrup to stand for 1 hour.

3 Squeeze all the lemons and measure out about 2 cups juice, making up the quantity with water if necessary. Cut the top third off each orange and carefully squeeze out the juice from the bottom two-thirds. ⚠ Strain both lemon and orange juices together – you should have about 6 cups.

4 Remove all the remaining flesh from the orange cases (see Preparation). Put the orange cases and "lids" on a tray (see Cook's tip) and put into the freezer.

5 Choose a very large bowl that will fit into the freezer compartment of a refrigerator or fast-freeze compartment of a freezer.

6 Pour the orange and lemon juice into the bowl then strain in the sugar syrup and stir well.

7 Freeze the juice for about 4 hours,

INDEX

Picture credits
Martin Brigdale: 40, 42
Alan Duns: 4/5, 6, 18/19, 20/1, 22, 24, 25, 58, 66/7, 68, 70, 71
James Jackson: 50, 60/1, 62, 65, 75, 77
Michael Kay: 78/9, 81, 82
Chris Knaggs: 10/11, 12/13, 14, 30
Don Last: 45, 46/7, 48
Fred Mancini: 27, 28
Peter Myers: 17, 38, 39, 57, 64
Roger Phillips: 32, 34/5, 36, 52/3, 54/5
Paul Webster: 9
Paul Williams: 59